ENGLISH CERAMICS

JACKET FRONT A Chelsea figure, representing Pantaloon, from the Italian Comedy Series. The piece, made *circa* 1750, is in soft paste, and is four and a quarter inches high. *Frontispiece* Worcester jug of about 1760. It is nine inches high with mask lip and cabbage leaf embossment, and decorated with printed and painted rural scenes.

ENGLISH
CERAMICS

Earthenware ✦ Delft ✦ Stoneware
Cream-Ware ✦ Porcelain
Including a section on Welsh factories

by
Stanley W. Fisher, F.R.S.A.

HAWTHORN BOOKS, INC.
Publishers · New York

First American Edition, 1966

Printed in Great Britain

3420

CONTENTS

Acknowledgements

The author and publishers are indebted to the following for the excellent photographs used to illustrate this work:

Antique Porcelain Company Ltd. 10, 90, 91, 96, 97, 98, 99, 124, 125, 127, 138, 139, 145; Boswell & Ward 87; British Museum (Crown Copyright) 22, 24, 25, 26, 27, 50, 55, 56, 57, 58; A. Gresham Copeland, Esq. 67, 71, 167, 177; W. T. Copeland & Sons Ltd. 70, 169; Christie, Manson & Woods Ltd. 9, 85, 102, 104, 107, 147; Delomosne & Son 100, 158, 160, 168; Fitzwilliam Museum 93, 94, 95, 108; Mrs. Esme Godkin 126; Mintons Ltd. 118; William Morris Museum 173, 178; Nottingham Museum 3; Royal Doulton 45; Sotheby & Co. 33, 35, 40, 41, 86, 131, 134, 136; Swansea Museum 157; Victoria & Albert Museum (Crown Copyright) 7, 11, 28, 29, 30, 31, 37, 49, 109, 133, 156; Josiah Wedgwood & Sons Ltd. 8, 47, 48, 53, 54, 59, 60, 61, 62, 63, 64, 65, 66; Worcester Royal Porcelain Co. Ltd.; Colour Frontispiece, 110, 113, 118, 119, 128, 174.

INTRODUCTION

The fascination of 'old china' lies much deeper than in its un-doubted beauty, which itself is apparent in so many widely different styles, shapes, patterns and colours. It is true, of course, that serious collectors may fill their cabinets with specimens that are chosen, with these factors in mind, to make a glowing display of loveliness, but there are other aspects of collecting which appeal to different mentalities, even though the ultimate results may aesthetically reach the same conclusion. Thus, Lady Charlotte Schreiber, probably the most indefatigable (and fortunate) collector of all time, aimed simply to possess a specimen repre-sentative of every style of every ceramic-making factory – with the result that nothing could possibly surpass the beauty of the great collection that may still be seen in the Victoria and Albert Museum in London. Interest in ceramics may indeed take many forms.

The story of the early years of porcelain making in this country is itself fascinating – the attempts, some of them ludicrous, to copy the wonderful wares of the Chinese, the heartaches and the bankruptcies, the intrigue, the wanderings of the pioneer potters and decorators, and the occasional final triumphs, often by pure accident. The student of anthropology finds that in pottery and porcelain there is much to interest him, not only in the host of pieces made and decorated to commemorate notable events or personalities, but also in the development of the kinds of ware made in different countries, at different times, for different markets. He may ponder on the differences between and the contrasting virtues of, for instance, the mantelpiece ornaments made by Astbury (then sold for coppers but now worth hundreds of pounds) and the magnificent figures made at Chelsea for the London gentry. The story of ceramics is indeed the story of mankind.

There are many collectors who are properly appreciative of beauty but who are even more attracted by questions of technique, and in this regard the scope is virtually endless. Apart from the methods used in making the body of the ware, throwing on the wheel, casting, moulding, pressing, modelling and so on, it must then be decorated. Some pieces are so intrinsically lovely that they need little additional embellishment. Others may be painted in blue under the glaze, enamelled over it, splendidly gilded or, like the famous Wedgwood wares, covered with applied raised ornament in contrasting colours. Add to the almost unlimited permutations and combinations of these and other methods of decoration the use of printing by means of transfers as an aid to cheapness but nevertheless capable of producing lovely effects, and it is clear to see that the field of interest is extremely wide.

The urge to collect china is inspired in many ways, and one splendid collection of Nantgarw porcelain and English porcelain figures really began when a cheap china dog was bought for a few pence in a junk shop. Many begin to collect as a result of their interest in a few family treasures. Their value has probably always been exaggerated, and one day, it may be, a similar piece is seen in the window of an antique shop. Investigation follows, and whether or not a purchase is made, a desire is born to know more, and perhaps even to possess more. The questions then arise – 'What will it cost? How shall I learn more about it? Do I like it as well as that other piece on the top shelf?' And so forth.

Naturally enough one must distinguish between the serious collector and those who merely like to have attractive pieces around them, on the mantelpiece, standing on pieces of furniture. or hanging on the wall. A cabinet of porcelain, tastefully arranged, is a lovely sight and one of never-failing interest to collectors and to the ignorant alike, for of all collectable works of art, perhaps, china fits best into any scheme of home furnishing. It never dates, its colours blend, its interest is perennial, and its cost need not be excessive – even in these days when fuller appreciation of its virtues has led to high prices.

When once the 'collecting bug' has bitten, every visit to a new district or town, every holiday trip, is the opportunity to scour the antique shops in search of an addition to the collection. But in order to collect there must be knowledge which can lead to the joy of securing a bargain that is denied to the mere 'cheque book collector'. It is the purpose of this book to impart a grounding of that knowledge, which may later be supplemented and enlarged by the study of more advanced specialist literature, by visits to museums and dealers, and by the actual handling of, and argument about, specimens belonging to fellow collectors.

PLATE I **Early British Pottery (page 10). The pottery of the Ancient-British period is conveniently divided into four main classes, Cinery Urns, Drinking Cups, so-called Food Vessels, and Immolation Urns intended to hold the ashes of sacrificed infants. All are crudely modelled, with little assistance from the potter's wheel, of lightly and imperfectly baked local clay, decorated according to the potter's untutored whim. As time passed shapes became more sophisticated, and one occasionally finds an attempt at careful modelling, usually of human figures or animal forms.**

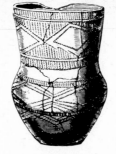

Ancient British Pottery

Anglo-Saxon Cinery Urns

Mediæval "Pottes" and Jugs

Liquor Vessel
(Probably 12th Century)

I

A SHORT HISTORY
OF CERAMICS

There is no record of the early beginnings of the craft of making vessels of clay for use as food or drink containers – of the early progression through the stages of baking in the sun, firing in a kiln, shaping by hand, throwing on a primitive potter's wheel, glazing to secure imperviousness to liquids, and decorating at the potter's untutored whim. It is clear, however, that at some time or other, at different periods in different countries, the early kiln-baked clays which we call earthenwares were improved upon in different ways. Thus, an earthenware made of some kind of natural clay was subjected to a much higher kiln temperature to become stoneware – a much harder vitrified material which was impervious to water – while the addition of other substances, notably china-clay (kaolin) and china-stone (petuntse) was found to give the translucency which is the distinguishing feature of porcelain. Certain non-porosity and added beauty was given by a protecting layer of glaze (or glass), which was probably an early Egyptian invention, and which is found with few exceptions upon all three bodies – earthenware, stoneware and porcelain.

In our own country the Romans made much fine pottery, but on their departure the craft was continued only by itinerant potters, of whom we have no record, who worked wherever they found suitable clay until local needs had been supplied. This medieval pottery was usually clumsy, often misshapen, and covered with a lead glaze in green, brown or yellow. Decoration was mainly incised (or scratched), impressed, or applied in the form of shaped pads of clay. Apparently the potter used for this purpose anything that came to hand, bits of twig, sea-shells, nails and so on, but some innate sense of craftsmanship and design always prevented him from obscuring the plastic nature of the clay. There were of course no decorators, as we understand the term, in those days.

It was during the fifteenth century that potteries were established at many centres, among them London, Wrotham in Kent, in Staffordshire, Derbyshire and Cheshire. Decoration in colour was introduced, notably in the form of applied decoration in contrasting colours which led up to the popularity of what are known as *slip wares* in the seventeenth century. This kind of pottery, which is associated particularly with a family of Staffordshire potters by the name of Toft, is to-day rare and valuable. It has no delicacy and was never intended to be other than utilitarian. The simple process of manufacture was that upon a red clay body a mixture of white clay and water (*slip* as we call it) was worked into patterns of wavy and dotted lines, flowers and leaves, animals and birds, and crude human figures and busts, before the whole was covered with lead glaze. Many important pieces bear names which may be either those of the makers or of intended recipients.

Towards the end of the seventeenth century, as some faint glimmerings of Far-Eastern culture began to spread to Europe, a handful of potters began to experiment with stoneware, in imitation of the ware then being made by a Meissen (Dresden) potter named Johann Böttger, who in turn had already copied from the Chinese. The best known of them are John Dwight of Fulham, who perfected a lovely white stoneware, and John and David Elers, whose red or black ware was lathe-turned in formal geometrical patterns, or else bore applied ornament which had been stamped out in metal dies. This *sprigged* decoration was developed to a high degree by John Astbury, an early eighteenth-century potter who worked very much in the Elers style, though his ware was glazed whereas Astbury's was not.

Though no glaze was really needed on stoneware, another class of seventeenth-century ware is known by the name of *salt-glazed*, because it was glazed with salt thrown into the kiln at a temperature of over two thousand degrees Fahrenheit; this resulted in the characteristic, slightly pitted, orange-skin appearance. The white surface of the early ware was sometimes enhanced by the addition of incised design which was then filled in with blue pigment. Stoneware was further developed right into the eighteenth century, culminating in a spate of colourful, jewel-like enamelling in the Chinese and continental styles, but at the same time lead-glazed pottery was improved to a high degree. Whieldon made figures and also perfected the use of mingled glazes in different colours in what are known as his 'tortoiseshell' wares. While with Wedgwood he used a fine green glaze on moulded articles such as the well-known 'cauliflower' tea-pots and tea-caddies, on which it contrasted to perfection with the creamy-white body. During the eighteenth century, too, Ralph Wood of Burslem followed the Astbury tradition in the making of mantelpiece figures and the familiar Toby Jug – to be followed by his descendants and many others who developed the Staffordshire Figures which are so popular today.

Early in the eighteenth century began attempts at imitating Chinese porcelain; this resulted in the making of what is known as delft in Holland and in our own country, majolica in Italy and Spain, and faïence in Germany and France. The only similarity between porcelain and delft lay in the white surface colour of each and in the kind of decoration, in Chinese style, which was applied to it, for whereas porcelain is translucent, delft is not, being merely ordinary earthenware covered with a white tin-oxide based glaze, the powdery texture of which demanded bold, unhesitant brushwork. We speak of the 'delft painter's touch' when we consider this kind of necessarily crude decoration, which is to be found upon the delft made between about 1600 and 1770 at London, Bristol and Liverpool.

PLATE 2 Toft Ware Charger. A typical example of Toft Ware, dating from about 1660–80. The amusing decoration is in brown slip on a yellow-brown body, and features the characteristically applied name of (probably) its maker, the trellissed border, and the rudimentary drawing of what was intended to be a cavalier.

PLATE 3 Medieval 'Mask-Lip' Jug. This fourteenth-century jug is made of brown clay, with applied decoration in darker brown, and covered with a greenish-yellow lead glaze which stops short of the base by several inches. The mask-lip, with its staring eyes, is the ▼ ancestor of the eighteenth-century lips of Worcester 'cabbage-leaf'.

PLATE 5 **Salt-glazed Loving Cups.** The date of these white salt-glazed loving-cups is fixed by the inscription, *1754 EB*, upon the larger one. Both are decorated in the *sgraffito* style with 'scratch-blue' designs. The thinness of potting, the graceful shapes, and the restrained decoration are typical of the best kind of early salt-glazed wares. ▲

PLATE 6 **Astbury Teapot and Stand** A typical example of Astbury ware made about 1740. The body is red, and the decoration was impressed upon pads of white clay previously applied to receive it. The addition of the lead glaze, when fired, then gave a warm, brownish colour to the red body, and 'sprigged' decoration became cream-coloured. ▼

◄

PLATE 4 **Stoneware Tankard.** This large tankard, nine inches high, was made at Fulham about 1770. The pitted, orange-skin surface-texture of the salt glaze can be clearly seen, and the colour merges from dark brown to buff in typical style. The applied decoration suggests that the vessel was probably made for use by bell-ringers.

So far as translucent porcelain proper is concerned, it is known that certain continental potters experimented successfully as early as 1580, but not until 1710 was anything done on a large scale; it was at Meissen that Böttger found out that the true porcelain of the Far East was composed of a mixture of china-clay and china-stone. Then, in 1745, the chemists at Vincennes evolved their own kind of porcelain, an imitation made of china-clay and a *fritt* of powdered glass which we now call *soft paste* or 'artificial' porcelain. It was this kind of substitute which our own potters, working independently and without any kind of Royal or State patronage, one by one invented. At Bow, Thomas Frye and Edward Heylyn took out a patent in 1744 and a factory was established at Chelsea perhaps even a little earlier. These were followed soon after 1750 by rival concerns at Bristol, Worcester, Derby, Lowestoft, Liverpool and Longton Hall in Staffordshire – all making soft-paste porcelains of different compositions. Then, in 1768, William Cookworthy found out how to make true porcelain, probably quite by accident, and set up a factory in Plymouth which was later moved to Bristol and finally, so far as its 'secrets' and methods were concerned, to New Hall in the Potteries.

Every now and then idealists tried with varying degrees of success to market new *pastes* (bodies) which were better than the others. Thus, in the 1820's, William Billingsley, chemist and china-painter, invented a wonderfully beautiful paste which he made at Pinxton, Nantgarw and Swansea until at length ruinous kiln losses brought failure and a return to the old position of paid decorator in another's factory. The same kind of attempts were made elsewhere, resulting often in unrivalled beauty and technical perfection but in bankruptcy also. The established factories introduced paste after paste, always striving after perfection, until with all the resources of the great potting centre of Staffordshire behind them, Spodes perfected and introduced, soon after 1800, a new body in which china-clay and china-stone were reinforced with calcined bone or *bone-ash*. It was not long before variations of this new paste had replaced every other kind, and there has been little change in its composition since.

When our potters first made porcelain they had no previous experience in the decorating of it, for the old styles which suited earthenware were quite unsuited to the much more delicate ware. It is true that now and again, on Liverpool wares in particular, we recognise the bold brushwork of a delft painter, but by and large the decoration on early English porcelain was the result of a new technique, and the popular styles were copied from alien sources. At first, because Chinese porcelain was so popular and familiar, at least among the educated and well-to-do, decoration was carried out in the Chinese style, in blue or in enamels. Occasionally the exotic Oriental designs were exactly copied, but more usually the separate motifs, the mandarin figures, the flowering shrubs, the dragons, the pagodas and so on were used in endless combinations to form the kind of patterns which Europeans expected to see. The much hackneyed *Willow Pattern*, though of later date, is a typical example of the kind of decoration which no Chinese artist could possibly ever perpetrate. Very few Japanese patterns were copied, apart from those in the style of a seventeenth-century potter named Kakiemon, which may be seen on Worcester and Bow porcelains in particular, under such nicknames as 'wheatsheaf', 'banded hedge', 'quail' and 'partridge'.

From the famous Meissen factory, on the outskirts of Dresden, much fine porcelain was exported to England, and its designs (many of which were adaptations of Chinese originals) were copied by our decorators between about 1760 and 1770 while at the same time the Oriental taste fell gradually into disfavour. The German styles which quickly became popular include European landscapes and harbour scenes and naturalistic birds; but above all the greatest influence on British porcelain decoration was in the forms of flowers and the wonderfully colourful, entirely imaginary creatures known as 'exotic birds', which at Worcester, rendered in different styles by innumerable artists, were reserved upon scale-blue grounds to splendidly brilliant effect. The flower painting took three distinct forms, formal Oriental flowers

PLATE 7 Whieldon Teapot. This well-shaped teapot, made about 1765, is sharply moulded in the Chinese style which was so popular at that time. The lovely lead glazes of yellow, green and brown are not confined in any way to the lines of the moulded decoration. Notice the typical shapes of the handle and spout, and the neatly fitting lid. The teapot was made *circa* 1765 and is five and a quarter inches high.

PLATE 9 Ralph Wood Toby Jug. This beautifully modelled jug was made by Ralph Wood Senior between 1760 and 1770, and is named 'The Squire'. Notice the clear-cut, detailed features, and try to visualise the glowing beauty of the coloured glazes used by Ralph Wood on all his models. The separate top of the hat, which formed a drinking vessel, is missing.

PLATE 8 Wedgwood 'Cauliflower' Teapot. This beautiful teapot may be dated about 1750. The modelling is of the highest quality, and the lower half is green-glazed on a cream-ware body. A green glaze derived from copper was known in the Middle Ages, but after centuries of disuse it was re-introduced and perfected by Wedgwood when he was working with Whieldon.

PLATE 10 Bow Candlesticks. These candlesticks each have the figures of a hunting couple resting under green foliage. The male figures hold guns, and the females hold birds. Each group also contains a dog. The principal colours are puce, green and blue. The height of both is twelve inches, and they date from about 1760.

(*indianische Blumen*), naturalistic flowers (*Streu Blumen*), and bouquets and sprigs of idealised flowers (*Meissner Blumen*).

During the time of this predominance of the German styles it was inevitable that the influence of the second great continental factory at Sèvres should occasionally have some effect on English design, and when the Meissen concern was taken over by the Prussians in 1763 the resultant disorganisation gave the French their chance to oust their rivals as dictators of fashion in porcelain decoration. The effect, between about 1770 and the end of the century, is seen on our wares in the shape of a spate of wonderful

20

ground (all-over) colours such as *bleu-de-roi*, *bleu céleste* (turquoise), apple, pea and sea-greens, and *Rose Pompadour* (claret), allied often to magnificent gilded patterning of every kind. We see too, on Chelsea, Derby and Worcester wares in particular, a great variety of daintily gay arrangements of floral and foliate festoons, seen to typical effect in the Worcester 'hop trellis' patterns.

Porcelain decoration after 1800, when there was marked acceleration of the change from individuality to commercialism, is too vast and complex a subject to be adequately described in these pages. With technical difficulties more or less overcome there

PLATE 11 Worcester Heart-shaped Dish. A lovely example of exotic-bird painting in the style of Evans and Aloncle of Sèvres, probably by an outside decorator, allied to a gilt-scrolled border of pea-green, dating from the period *circa* **1770-75. The beautifully painted background is particularly noticeable, and the insects and birds are drawn in wonderful detail and are perfectly placed.**

was no limit to possible extravagance in decoration, and extra-vagance was in fact often welcomed by a new kind of public who could afford the best and who wanted its value to be obvious. The porcelain body was used more and more merely as a canvas to receive fine painting in every conceivable style, and though sometimes the older, still-flourishing factories such as Derby and Worcester carried on their old traditions of restrained design, even in their wares technical perfection may sometimes seem a poor exchange for the inexplicable but real attraction of their imperfect early productions – at least in the eyes of the collector. At the beginning, of course, few factories had their own staff of proficient, trained decorators, and special or difficult work was often entrusted to 'outside decorators' in London or elsewhere, whereas every nineteenth-century factory of any importance had its own properly trained artists, many of them specialists, and many of them known to us by their styles and, sometimes, by their names. The result is that the collector of later wares must perforce be interested more in decoration than in the paste upon which it rests, particularly since this was more or less standardised throughout the industry.

2

TECHNIQUES OF
THE POTTER

Pottery making is among the most ancient of all crafts, and essentially among the simplest. Indeed, in early times there is no doubt that the housewife made her own crude vessels from a substance which is everywhere abundant, and only when pottery making was divorced from everyday life and was adapted to factory processes were difficulties encountered, due to the endless experiment with new materials and new processes which was essential to survival.

The earliest pieces of pottery were probably shaped entirely by hand without any kind of mechanical aid, either by *pinching* or by *coiling*. In the first process a ball of clay was taken, and the thumb was forced into it almost to the base, so that by evenly pinching with hand and thumb, while rotating the ball, the sides of the vessel were made thinner and thinner. The second method was more suitable for larger vessels, and made use of long thin rods of clay, rolled out by hand on a flat surface, which were then used to build up the shape in coils, splicing when necessary, on a slab base or a coiled one like a catherine-wheel. The outside and inside of the completed vessel were then smoothed with the fingers.

At some later date, but still before the coming of factory methods, three distinct ways of potting were evolved, which are still used today. They are *throwing*, *pressing* (or *moulding*), and *casting*. Throwing is done upon what must be one of the very

23

earliest forms of machinery, the potter's wheel, in its simplest form merely a revolving head on a spindle, turned by any convenient means. Even today, in the Far East and in India wheels are turned by spinning the heavy head by means of a stick applied to holes around it, and on the continent *kick wheels*, with a heavy flywheel low down which is kicked round by the feet, have been used from the beginnings of the craft. Later developments are many, and include the still popular crank and kick-bar mechanism, many types of gearing and, of course, the modern power drive. Whatever the driving power the principle is the same. A piece of prepared, soft clay, thoroughly mixed and rendered free from air pockets, is thrown down firmly on to the centre of the wheel, and as it spins the potter works it up and down between his hands in a cylindrical mass until he is satisfied that it is uniformly soft. He then opens it out with his thumbs, and uses his skill to make a vessel of the desired form. Nothing seems so simple to the onlooker, but the beginner strives in vain until his mass of clay has mysteriously dissolved away in slush.

When the thrower has made his vessel he cuts it away from the wheel by passing a wire under its base, and it can then be finished in several ways, if indeed any kind of additional finish is needed. For example, very large vessels may be thrown in separate sections to be joined together when partly dried by the use of slip. The rough form from the wheel may be placed in a mould and carefully pressed into it to be removed easily later, because clay

PLATE 12 Worcester Vase. During the latter part of the nineteenth century the Worcester management were ever on the search for new styles of decoration, and the new 'ivory' body was ideal for the production of ware in what was called the 'Japanesque' style. This vase is one of a series which was made to illustrate the manufacture of porcelain in Japan, and it is interesting to see the crude manner in which the potter's wheel was turned. The entire decoration is carried out in bronzes of various tints.

shrinks as it dries. If a very exact or smooth finish is desired, the vessel is allowed to dry in a warm place until it is 'leather hard', when it is carefully centred on the wheel, or placed in a special lathe, to be finished with turning tools. The base of nearly every tea-pot, bowl, saucer and so on has been finished by this process, and such is the individuality of the potter (and apparently of some of our early potteries) that the shape of foot-rim sections is often of great help in deciding where a doubtful piece was made.

The first step in pressing is to prepare suitable moulds, which are nowadays made of plaster of Paris, but which in the past have been made, and sometimes still are made, from clay, metal, wood, and even alabaster. Some moulds are in one piece, and others are in sections to allow easy withdrawal. Into these moulds thin sheets, or *bats* of moist clay are firmly pressed. When the clay has dried (and contracted) it may be released from the mould, which is taken apart if in sections, trimmed, and finished with modelling tools. Intricate pieces, such as figures or groups, may have to be moulded in many separate parts, which are then fixed together with slip, and it is interesting to know that the skilled operator who used to be responsible for this work in the eighteenth century was called a 'repairer'.

The process of casting seems to have been invented in the Potteries, probably in an attempt to make early eighteenth-century stoneware vessels as thin as possible. As in pressing, a mould is prepared, but of some absorbent material such as plaster of Paris, into which slip is poured. Since the mould absorbs the water in the slip, a coating of clay collects upon its inner wall, and it is kept full of slip until the deposit is of the required thickness, when the surplus is poured away. Quite clearly by this method very thin and delicate ware may be made, its thinness limited only by difficulty of handling.

When an earthenware or porcelain vessel has been shaped by any of these methods it is allowed to dry, and it must then be fired. In primitive times pottery was simply baked in a bonfire, but the use of some kind of oven or kiln, whether fired by wood, coal, gas or electricity superseded such a crude method very early on. The question of kiln temperatures is clearly too technical to discuss here, and it must suffice to say that this varies with every different kind of ceramic body, from comparatively low temperatures for earthenware to much higher ones for stoneware and porcelain. True porcelains were fired at a greater heat than artificial ones, and the correct definition of the former is that they were fired at a 'harder' (higher) temperature than their imitations, rather than that they are necessarily harder to the touch.

If we except the tin-glazed and salt-glazed wares mentioned in the previous chapter, so far as our own ceramics are concerned the fired body, when in what we call the 'biscuit' state, must receive a coat of a mixture generally rich in lead oxide which will, when fired, cover the ware with a thin layer of glass. This layer may be colourless or, as in the case of the glazes used by Whieldon and Ralph Wood, it may be stained with oxides of manganese, copper, iron and cobalt to give browns, greens, reds and blues. The application of an ordinary glaze may be by dipping, brushing, sponging, sprinkling or, as was sometimes done by the Chinese, by spraying through a piece of gauze. When the glaze is dry, its water content having been absorbed by the porous biscuit body, the piece is ready for firing in what is known as a *glost kiln*, the temperature of which is lower than that of the biscuit kiln.

In its unfired state the glaze is extremely vulnerable, and all kinds of devices have been used to prevent the finished piece from being marked. Plates, for example, must clearly be kept apart, and one of the characteristics of early Chelsea porcelain is the presence underneath plates or dishes of three or four tiny little blemishes which show where they rested upon tiny clay *spurs*. Many an early piece of our porcelain is disfigured by black specks or smoky patches, the result of smoke from the fuel used to fire the glost kiln, despite the customary use of *saggers*, or boxes of fireclay, in which the ware was placed; their shape and size varied to suit the various kinds of ware. In fact, the spotless purity of modern ware is a tribute to the long experiment that has gone into the making of the perfect sagger, though we must not forget, also, that the electric kiln has solved many problems.

Fine decoration in colour has always been an aim of china makers, who have been hindered by the fact that not all metallic pigments would withstand the high temperatures necessary to re-melt the glaze, even though those of the *enamelling kiln* are lower than those of the glost kiln. Thus, while colours may be applied either under or over the glaze the only colour which could be used under it by our early porcelain makers was *under-glaze blue*, derived from cobalt oxide; every other pigment had to be applied over the fired glaze, in the form of enamels prepared by mixing mineral substances with soft flux or glass. A further problem (which often led to unexpected and occasional wonderful results in Chinese potteries) was that final colour is dependent upon kiln temperatures and atmospheric conditions. That is why oxide of iron, for example, can be used to give a wide range of colours from yellow, through light and dark brown, to red and purple.

The most obvious method of applying coloured decoration is by means of a brush, but there are of course many other methods.

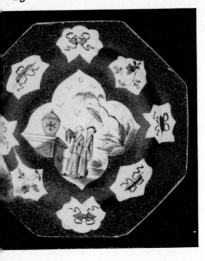

13

14

15

In the ordinary way, all-over ground colours may be applied
with a brush, but among the most effective kinds of underglaze
blue styles on early porcelain is that known as *powder blue*,
favoured particularly at Worcester, Caughley, Lowestoft and
Bow. The technique was a Chinese one in which the pigment,
in powder form, was blown upon the ware through a tube,
closed with gauze at one end. Any intended *reserves* (or spaces
left white to receive decoration) were masked. Masking was used
also to pattern our early nineteenth-century *silver resist* lustred
ware.

During the latter half of the eighteenth century pottery and
porcelain of good quality and aesthetic merit was no longer the
sole prerogative of the well-to-do, one of the reasons for this
being the introduction of transfer printing as a means of decoration; being a mechanical process it was so much quicker and
cheaper than painting. Printing by means of paper transfers taken
from engraved copper plates was done at the Battersea enamelling
works as early as 1753, and the process was adopted at Worcester
and Liverpool within three years, the men responsible being
Robert Hancock and John Sadler respectively. The first printing
was in overglaze form, mostly in black enamel, but again within
a few years the Worcester management, in answer to the demand
for more and more imitations of the Chinese *Blue Nankin* wares,
introduced printing in underglaze blue, to be quickly followed by
the Caughley, Liverpool and Lowestoft concerns. Then, towards

the end of the century, a new technique was perfected, in which stippled prints were applied to the ware from bats of glue, instead of from paper transfers. The results are known as *bat printing*, and the process differs from ordinary transfer printing in that oil was used instead of the colour, which was applied in powder form to the tacky surface.

Printing in colours was always the aim of early ceramic technicians who had at first to be content with using ordinary outline prints which could be washed in with enamels. This washing-in could be done carefully, as in the case of certain early Worcester mandarin patterns in the Chinese style, or in the clumsy, haphazard way which is evident on much late eighteenth-century earthenware. Spodes, in particular, made the best of the washing-in method, using one print to produce many different versions according to colouring; but the first significant method of colour-printing proper was introduced by the Pratts of Fenton, who in the mid-nineteenth century, just in time for the Great Exhibition, used sets of transfers, each printing a different colour, to decorate their famous Pot Lids. Finally, the invention of lithography, coincident with the invention of many new pigments capable of resisting high kiln temperatures, made it possible to use colour transfers as we understand them today.

It is important to understand that decoration by means of transfers should not be despised by reason of its mechanical nature. Its introduction brought well-designed and well-decorated wares within the reach of everybody, and the work of a skilled engraver is often preferable to the brushwork of an indifferent artist.

Whatever the method used to decorate a piece of earthenware or porcelain, the effect is enhanced by the use of gilding in one form or another. In its early form, as used at Longton Hall for example, gold leaf was applied to the ware with japanners size, but since it was unfired it would not withstand washing or constant use, and the gilding upon most of our early wares is of the kind known as *honey gilding*. By this method gold leaf was mixed with honey, which of course was lost in the kiln to leave behind a dull gold that could be burnished or chased with a metal tool. Then, about 1790, came the mercury-amalgam process, in which mercury replaced the honey. It was easier, but the results are much brassier and flatter, lacking the soft, rich appearance of the old honey gilding.

Of intent, methods of ornamentation other than the application of colour have not been discussed in this chapter, since so many of them apply in particular to specific kinds of ware, which will receive proper attention in the following pages.

3

MAKING A COLLECTION

It is impossible to be interested in ceramics without longing to collect them or to place any limit upon the size of a collection when once begun. Interest is something which is aroused in so many ways – the possession of a few family pieces, a visit to a museum or a great house open to the public, a new friendship with a collector, or even the casual reading of an article in a magazine. But much of the real attraction of collecting, however begun, is derived from the search for specimens and from the ways in which the fullest benefit can be had from them when they are found and assembled.

It would be presumptuous for me or for anyone else, however expert or devoted, to dictate to a beginner as to what he ought to collect, for beauty is subjective, and one man's meat is another man's poison. Many collectors have begun by collecting any and every piece which appeals and which seems reasonably priced, but most become specialists in the end, whether in pieces from some particular factory, in a particular style or of a certain period, or decorated in some particular manner. There is a wide choice, and a wide range of prices, for though rarity, age and quality govern value, much that is worthwhile is still comparatively inexpensive.

Let us admit that only the experienced collector can hope, nowadays, to pick up bargains in a junk shop, a general antique shop, or at an auction sale. Every small concern, however remote, is regularly scoured by larger dealers, and no country sale is neglected by them. Nevertheless, as knowledge increases, not only of specimens themselves but also of their current market values, it is sometimes possible to buy more reasonably in a provincial general shop than in London or in a recognised antiques centre. I have often been drawn into a discussion as to whether it is better to buy at auctions rather than from the trade. The conclusion is, that it all depends. At Sothebys or Christies, for example, a typical mixed sale of ceramic offers such as wide choice that although goods of exceptional quality will always command very high prices, the more ordinary ones, though still worthwhile and desirable, may often be bought reasonably. In contrast, at a country general sale too many people are trying to buy too few goods, a good piece stands out like a sore thumb, and prices are invariably sky-high. Furthermore, and above all, should a purchase turn out later to be broken, skillfully restored, or not what it was claimed to be in the catalogue, the buyer has no redress under the terms of the sale, while a dealer of repute is always willing to take back anything which later proves not what it was claimed to be. That is the position, and it may be added only that if one decides to buy at an auction sale, a firm limit must be made in the light of current prices, and not exceeded however great the temptation. It is better, in fact, if one is likely to be carried away by enthusiasm, to leave a bid with the auctioneer, and to forget all about it.

I would repeat that unless and until a beginner has gained knowledge he should not expect to buy cheaply in a general antique shop. If for no other reason than that a single piece of porcelain standing alone on a chest of drawers is probably priced high above its true value by the proprietor, who may not have had anything like it for years. On the other hand a specialist will have many comparable pieces in his stock, properly priced. They have to be, for otherwise he would be out of business. The wise collector, therefore, is willing to buy from such a dealer, confident that what he buys is what it is claimed to be, and paying not only for the article but also for the seller's knowledge, the trouble he has taken to find his specimens, and the guarantee that goes without saying. When once a reputable dealer has the confidence of his customer he will help him to find the sort of pieces he ought to have, at the right price, and he will tactfully guide his attention away from anything that is unworthy of 'The Collection'.

So much for buying. And in this connection it is remarkable what a difference is sometimes made to an apparently clean piece when it has been properly washed. The glaze of a soft-paste porcelain, in particular, is always somewhat scratched, and the scratches collect dirt. 'Scrubbs Ammonia' gently rubbed over the surface with cotton wool completely removes every trace of it, after which a soaking in any good washing-up liquid completes the treatment. Figures must be washed with a large hogshair artist's brush in the same sort of liquid with a little ammonia added, rinsed in clean tepid water, and set aside to dry on a piece of blotting paper. Otherwise, the bocage or any protruding arm or leg are liable to be broken.

A collection must be properly displayed. Some pieces are so large that they can only be placed upon pieces of furniture, vases high up and out of danger and bowls and dishes on steady flat surfaces, but otherwise cabinets are essential. Never overcrowd. The result is unsightly and even dangerous. A shallow cabinet is preferable, but a deeper one may be improved by making additional stepped shelves in the form of long hardwood boxes, covered with the same material as the back of the cabinet. This material should preferably be plain or at least indistinctly patterned in the same colour, which may be light buff or pale green unless one collects black ware, in which case yellow is essential. As regards shelving, wood is safe, but plate glass makes interior lighting much easier to arrange, since a strong overhead light, which can easily be ventilated, will shine right throughout the cabinet from top to bottom, but they must be well supported.

Arrangement is most important. It is unwise to allow plates to rest unsupported against the back of the cabinet, for sooner or later they will slip forward with dire results. Stands for these and for cups and saucers are cheaply obtainable and are best made from white plastic-covered wire. Dishes and plates do indeed form an effective background to other pieces, which should be arranged to avoid monotony. Thus, tall pieces such as tea or coffee-pots, tankards, teapots and vases should alternate with cups and saucers or bowls. Bowls look best on high shelves, but openwork baskets or handled trays are seen to best advantage at the bottom of the cabinet. 'Blue and white' does not live amicably with polychrome wares, and figures are best in their own cabinet.

An interesting collection deserves a good catalogue, preferably loose-leaved, with entries under the headings of catalogue number, attribution, description and date, mark, date and place of purchase, cost price and, if possible, a photograph. Indeed, the photography of one's specimens is fascinating in itself, the only essential being a camera which will take good 'close-ups'. Lens speed is unimportant, since the subject will not move. Photography in the open air is best, so avoiding troublesome highlights and reflections, but good results (and a constant exposure speed) may be obtained indoors by the use of two carefully placed 150 watt bulbs in suitable reflectors.

Labels should be numbered according to the catalogue. Self adhesive ones are excellent, and to avoid trouble when washing the object they may be treated with transparent varnish. There is something to be said for having one's name printed on the labels. Who knows? One day labelled pieces from 'The John Smith Collection' may be in great demand, for the labels upon pieces from such collections as the Trapnell or Wallace Elliot are never on any account removed by their later fortunate owners. Labels may bear also the name of the responsible factory and the date of manufacture, but care must be taken to keep them of such a size that they can be placed on smaller pieces.

Finally, every collection should be separately insured, with an up-to-date inventory prepared and certified by a recognised expert as the basis of the policy. The cost is not too high, and financial recompense for damage or loss is better than nothing.

4

COLLECTORS' MISTAKES

I have yet to meet a collector who claims never to have made a bad purchase, and every one of us has profited by mistakes; these may have been of several different kinds – falling for convenience into three categories: forgeries, fakes and restorations.

A forgery, as far as we are concerned, is a piece which is a copy of an original piece of pottery or porcelain, made with the intention of deceiving, or being likely to deceive the purchaser. Bearing in mind the fact that the forger chooses valuable wares as his models, there is a large class of imitation Derby, Bow and Chelsea figures, and of fine Worcester porcelain, which was made from 1845 onwards by Messrs. Samson & Co. of Paris. The potting, modelling and decoration was always first class, and at a distance they are difficult to fault. They are so good indeed that they are now collected, but whereas the originals were made of soft paste, the imitations are of continental true porcelain, with the result that the paste is much colder in tone, the enamels (and the mark, if any) stand out harshly on the surface instead of sinking into the glaze, and the gilding is brilliantly brassy. It was claimed by Samsons that it was their custom to add a distinguishing mark of their own, but be that as it may, their efforts still continue to deceive many collectors who should know better.

Among the most highly prized Chelsea wares are certain little cream jugs, bearing mounding in relief in the shape of a goat and a bee, and recognised as being extremely early productions of the

PLATE 18 Samson's 'Derby' Figure. Though apparently a Derby model and bearing a Derby mark, this figure was in fact made towards the end of the nineteenth century by Samson of Paris; made of 'hard paste' it is, however, exquisitely modelled and enamelled.

factory. Copies of these rarities, and of others including pea-pods and tureens in the shape of cabbage lettuces, were made at Coalport. Again, the paste, though soft, is harder than it ought to be; it is dead white instead of creamy, and its translucency against an electric light is colourless instead of pale yellow with tiny pin-holes or specks of greater translucency.

Much more deceptive are many pieces of Coalport porcelain made after the great china painter and chemist Billingsley went there from Nantgarw, introducing a variety of his own beautiful paste which was never finally discarded. Add to this the facts that the same or similar moulds to those of the Welsh factories were used, that copper plates used for printing the Swansea mark were in the possession of the factory, and that painting by the same hand is to be found on wares from all the three factories, and it must be clear why many a piece of Coalport has been bought in the belief that it was made in Wales.

There are certain forgeries which ought not to deceive, but which do sometimes trap the careless. The well-known *pine-cone* or *strawberry* pattern found on much early Worcester printed in underglaze blue was extensively copied on wares made at some factory or other during the last quarter of the nineteenth century, but the presence of an intricate mark incorporating the Worcester crescent should prevent any deception. Similarly, although Booths of Tunstall, working at about the same time, made lovely copies of both *blue and white* and polychrome Worcester wares, the fact that they were made of light, opaque earthenware should be protection enough. It is unfortunately inevitable that so long as early porcelain is valuable, attempts will be made to deceive, and that with increasing technical knowledge such attempts will be more dangerous. Quite recently, in fact, there have appeared on the market, even in the sale rooms, some wonderfully clever imitations of Chelsea and Derby figures of the rarer kind. They are well-nigh perfect, they were made to deceive, and it is fortunate indeed that their very perfection and supposed rarity takes them out of reach of all but the wealthy.

Because earthenware is opaque, and can be judged only by surface appearance, a good forgery of a piece of saltglaze, an Astbury figure, or a Ralph Wood Toby is difficult to detect, and it is impossible to suggest any rule-of-thumb test. Indeed, not so long ago several authorities of world-wide repute were able to expose two small figures as forgeries only because, being exactly similar, they bore two entirely different impressed marks. Of course, again, this kind of forgery is unlikely to come the way of the small collector, who is more likely to be tempted by less costly and more crudely made imitations. Forged lustred Sunderland bowls, jugs and mugs are plentiful, but they are too obviously fresh, clean and untouched by time to be true. Similarly, it was not so long ago that an unscrupulous dealer could buy ordinary lustre jugs by the barrel, for a few pence apiece, and here again they are betrayed by their pristine appearance, and by a roughness of surface, particularly of the base inside the foot-rim, that is not present on the genuine article. The beginner should beware, too, of forged Staffordshire 'cottages', which by far outnumber the old.

A fake is any genuine piece which has been altered or added to with fraudulent intention. Thus, genuine eighteenth-century specimens of undecorated porcelain, or pieces sparsely decorated, have had more splendid decoration added to them, or marks, or both. Fortunately, with very few exceptions, and for various technical reasons, the refiring necessary to fix the new decoration leaves behind certain betraying traces, in the shape of a dulled or bubbled glaze, extensive iridescence, or smoke staining. A distinction must be drawn between fakes of this kind and what are known as *clobbered* wares. A clobbered piece of blue and white has had enamels added to the design in an obvious manner, making no attempt to hide the original blue pigment, whereas a faked piece of the same simple, comparatively cheap ware may be elaborately painted and gilded in such a manner as completely to obscure it. However, apart from the usual signs of re-firing, it is sometimes possible to detect a tiny trace, somewhere in the design, of the underglaze blue peeping out from beneath the splendour. Many genuine specimens have quite good enamelled decoration, particularly in the forms of border patterns, which seem to cry aloud for something lovely in the centre. The faker has often obliged, but there are certain clues in the detection of this kind of fraud, such as added decoration which is out of character, and the absence of such signs of wear as slight scratching on the new enamels. Rarity is prized by the collector, and nothing is simpler to the faker than to add some kind of rare mark.

Modern restorations are the bane of the beginner in collecting, and sometimes of the expert. Until a few years ago any kind of repair or restoration revealed itself in due course when the new white enamel changed to dirty yellow. Besides, the unfired enamels were easily scratched with the point of a knife. With the invention of new enamels, some of them fired at a low temperature, this discoloration was prevented, but repairs could still be clearly seen beneath the rays of an ultra-violet lamp, since they showed up chalky white against an otherwise peach-coloured or violet surface. Now, however, the position is changed, for restorers have discovered enamels and 'glazes' which defeat the 'lamp'. This is no place to argue the pros and the cons of this kind of restoration, which admittedly prolongs the life of valuable pieces, and which is done in all good faith by the specialists. On the other hand, it is becoming increasingly difficult to view an auction sale of fine porcelain or pottery, and collectors are bound, eventually, to question the perfect state of an expensive piece when it is offered by a dealer who himself may be uncertain. That is the position, and fortunately this kind of repair is so expensive that it is usually done only to pieces in private ownership. As yet, the collector may still detect an ordinary repair or restoration by smelling, by looking for opaque patches in a translucent piece of porcelain, by observing the difference in sheen between true glaze and a substitute, by careful pricking with a sharp point and, above all, by gentle biting or tapping with the teeth, when a restored part will feel and sound dead and dull compared with the un-yielding, almost metallic hardness of a true glaze.

5

BRITISH AND OVERSEAS COLLECTIONS

Collecting as we now understand it is a comparatively modern development, for, apart from the cabinets of representative specimens on the premises of such pioneer concerns as Worcester and Spode, only a very few private connoisseurs were beginning to appreciate and to seek fine pieces of pottery and porcelain as late as the last quarter of the nineteenth century. Their names are now well known, and include such pioneer enthusiasts as Lady Charlotte Schreiber, Trapnell, Herbert Allen and Frank Lloyd, whose collections, fine by any standard, have either been dispersed or left to national museums, where they may still be admired and studied. Thus, in Britain, the Victoria and Albert Museum has the Schreiber and Herbert Allen Collections, and the British Museum has the Frank Lloyd, all of them fully described and illustrated in catalogues which are unfortunately out of print and scarce. Few British cities and larger towns lack museums, and most of them house collections of ceramics, well displayed and either of a general or specialised nature according to locality. In the Potteries one would expect to find a collection of Staffordshire wares second to none, and this is at Hanley. At Worcester the representative works collection has recently been supplemented and enriched by the Dyson Perrins specimens, Swansea and Nantgarw lovers may admire the Glynn Vivian Collection in the Swansea Museum, and the Wedgwood enthusiast makes a pilgrimage to the works collection at Etruria.

Birmingham has one of the finest collections of ceramics in the country; the great Cecil Higgins Collection is at Bedford; Spodes have their own collection; the finest collection of Worcester porcelain in the world, made by the late Rissik Marshall, is housed in the Ashmolean Museum at Oxford, and the Fitzwilliam Museum at Cambridge is the proud custodian of the Glaisher Collection of English Pottery. Among the lesser museums, of which there are too many to be listed, mention may be made of those at Cheltenham, Nottingham and Bristol; all have fine collections.

Apart from museums proper, there are innumerable private collections which may be seen, either in 'stately homes' open to the public, or in the houses of their owners by appointment. The collection at Rous Lench Court, near Alcester in Warwickshire, painstakingly and lovingly formed by Mr. T. Burn, is outstanding, as is the Wernher Collection at Luton Hoo, in Bedfordshire – hardly a great house but one containing fine porcelain which has been collected, much of it for everyday use, over the years. The British collector, and the visitor from overseas, has only to visit the museums, and there enquire from their curators as to the whereabouts of local private collections, in order to see a wealth of all that is best in our national wares, for every collector, by and large, loves nothing better than to share his enthusiasm with his fellows.

A very notable English collector and writer on ceramics recently said to me that so far as European collections of British ceramics are concerned, they are practically non-existent. On the whole this is very true, and indeed one can well understand that continental connoisseurs, familiar with the glories of Sèvres and Meissen, might well be somewhat blind to the attractions of our own imitations. In fact, much of the English porcelain to be found on the Continent would seem to be Derby, often mistakenly identified as Chelsea, and though there is at the moment the beginnings of an interest in our ceramics in Paris, the position is that the collector who travels in Europe can find comparatively few British specimens either to admire or to acquire.

Collections

My American readers will not need very much advice from me as to the whereabouts of our British pottery and porcelain in their own country. Nevertheless, for the benefit of my own countrymen who are less informed mention may be made of some of the outstanding collections. The wonderful Irwin Untermyer Collection is probably well-known because it is so beautifully pictured and exactly described and documented in the sumptuous catalogue published in London by Thames and Hudson. In the Art Institute of Chicago may be seen the specialised (and, again, well-catalogued) Stieglitz Collection of Worcester Porcelain, and at Covington, Louisiana, the Siegmund Katz Collection, destined for the Boston Museum of Fine Art, is rich in the early wares, especially Chelsea. The Colonial Williamsburg Museum must not be overlooked, since it houses the fine Kidd Collection of English Pottery and also the Kauffman Collection of early Chelsea. There is, too, a good representative display of English pottery, with some porcelain, at the Henry Francis Dupont Museum at Winterthur, Pa. The Wedgwood lover should know that there is an American Wedgwood Society, and that Mr. Harry Buten, of Merion, Pa., the author of several books on Wedgwood, has a fine private museum of the wares.

Many American museums have an enviable record as regards the organisation of exhibitions of British ceramics during the past twenty years, among them the New York Metropolitan Museum of Art and the Detroit Institute of Arts. The Manfield Collection is in the Governor's Palace at Williamsburg, Virginia, the Dunlap Collection in New York, and the Lucy D. Aldrich Collection at Providence, Rhode Island. We must mention the Burnap Collection of English Pottery (of which there is a very informative, well-illustrated catalogue, published in 1953) which is in the William Rockhill Nelson Gallery of Art in Kansas City. Other fine collections may be seen at the Montreal Museum of Art, the Los Angeles County Museum, the Art Institute of Chicago, and the Albany Institute of History and Art, to mention but several of those museums which are best known.

The fascination of our British wares is such that the collecting of them, in spite of the constant rise in prices and the increasing scarcity, is bound to spread to countries where until quite recently they have been almost unknown. We may quote as an example of this the sudden popularity, a few years ago, in Australia, of Bernard Moore porcelain, which of course is too 'modern' for the notice of most British collectors, but which nevertheless is most attractive and technically excellent. When once interest has been aroused by any kind of ware the desire is born to delve deeper, to study and collect earlier wares, and in Australia, as in many other countries, one or two good collections of British porcelains in particular are being formed, and will inevitably lead to widespread enthusiasm.

6

BIBLIOGRAPHY

A great deal of information may be gleaned from well-illustrated books on ceramics, provided that reading is supplemented with the handling of as many pieces as possible. The collector nowadays has a very wide choice of literature; some books are out-of-date but still valuable from the points of view of interest and pictures, and others have been written recently in the light of the latest knowledge. Some deal with ceramics in general, while some are specialised. In addition, while there are books such as this which endeavour to interest the beginner in particular, the expert is even better catered for by those which take elementary knowledge for granted. Most books can of course be borrowed from libraries, or from reluctant collector friends, but it is better for everyone to form his own library to which he can at any time refer. Many copies can be purchased second-hand, though it is true to say that few books about collecting have not doubled or trebled their original selling price if they are now out of print.

This short bibliography is a selection of those books which are obtainable for the most part at reasonable prices, and which I have found to be most useful. One or two are expensive, but are included because they are indispensable to the serious collector.

PORCELAIN

General

Burton, W. – *Porcelain, its Nature, Art and Manufacture* (1906)

Bibliography

Cook, C. – *Life and Work of Robert Hancock* (1948)

Fisher, S. W. – *English Blue and White Porcelain of the Eighteenth Century* (1947); *China Collector's Guide* (1959); *Decoration of English Porcelain* (1954); *British Pottery and Porcelain* (1962)

Godden, G. A. – *Victorian Porcelain* (1961)

Hackenbroch, Y. – *Chelsea and other English Porcelain* (1957)

Honey, W. B. – *Old English Porcelain* (1928)

Watney, B. – *English Blue and White Porcelain of the Eighteenth Century* (1963)

Specialised

Barrett, F. A. – *Worcester Porcelain* (1953); *Caughley and Coalport Porcelain* (1951)

Boney, K. – *Liverpool Porcelain* (1957)

Gilhespy, F. B. – *Derby Porcelain* (1961); *Crown Derby Porcelain* (1951)

Hayden, A. – *Spode and His Successors* (1925)

Hobson, R. L. – *Worcester Porcelain* (1910)

Hurlbutt, F. – *Bow Porcelain* (1926); *Bristol Porcelain* (1928); *Chelsea China* (1937)

John, W. D. – *Nantgarw Porcelain* (1948); *Swansea Porcelain* (1958)

King, W. – *Chelsea Porcelain* (1922)

Lane, A. – *English Porcelain Figures of the Eighteenth Century* (1961)

Mackenna, F. S. – *Champion's Bristol Porcelain* (1947); *Cookworthy's Plymouth and Bristol Porcelain* (1946); *Chelsea Porcelain, Triangle and Raised Anchor Wares* (1948); *Chelsea Porcelain, The Red Anchor Period* (1951); *Chelsea Porcelain, The Gold Anchor Period* (1952)

Marshall, H. R. – *Coloured Worcester Porcelain of the First Period* (1954)

Spelman, W. W. R. – *Lowestoft China* (1905)

Watney, B. – *Longton Hall Porcelain* (1957)

EARTHENWARE
General
Burnap, F. P. & H. C. – *Catalogue of the Collection* (1953)
Haggar, R. G. – *English Country Pottery* (1950)
Hayden, A. – *Chats on English Earthenware* (1909)
Rackham, B. – *Early Staffordshire Pottery* (1951)
Rhead, G. W. – *The Earthenware Collector* (1920)
Mediaeval
Rackham, B. – *Mediaeval English Pottery* – (1948)
Slipware
Lomax, C. J. – *Quaint Old English Pottery* (1909)
Delft
Garner, F. H. – *English Delftware* (1948)
Stoneware
Blacker, J. F. – *A.B.C. of English Salt Glaze Stoneware* (1922)
Creamware
Towner, D. – *English Cream-coloured Earthenware* (1957)
Lustre
John, W. D. – *Old English Lustre Pottery* (1951)
Staffordshire
Andrade, C. – *Astbury Figures* (1924)
Barnard, H. – *Chats on Wedgwood Ware* (1924)
Church, A. H. – *Josiah Wedgwood* (1908)
Haggar, R. G. – *Staffordshire Chimney Ornaments* (1955); *The Masons of Lane Delph* (1952)
Honey, W. B. – *Wedgwood Ware* (1948)

MARKS
The subject of marks is one which cannot be fully dealt with in any general book, and I have made only incidental reference to them. I have found the books listed below to be the most useful and up-to-date. That by Rhead is the only one which lists practically all of the marks used by Staffordshire potters working during the latter half of the nineteenth century, but it is of course long out of print, and difficult to obtain.

Bibliography

Cushion, J. P. and Honey, W. B. – *Handbook of Pottery and Porcelain Marks* (1956)

Godden, G. A. – *Encyclopædia of British Pottery and Porcelain Marks* (1964)

Rhead, G. W. – *British Pottery Marks* (1910)

Thorn, C. J. – *Handbook of Old Pottery and Porcelain Marks* (1947)
In addition, the several catalogues of the collections in the Victoria & Albert and British Museums are invaluable, though some are out of print for the moment, and difficult to obtain. The American collector in particular should try to obtain copies of the many catalogues of exhibitions held from time to time in such museums as the New York Metropolitan, the Montreal Museum of Art, The Institute of Chicago, and the Detroit Institute of Arts. There is a good choice of journals either devoted to the arts, or containing regular articles about antiques. These include *The Antique Collector, Apollo, Antique Dealer and Collectors' Guide, Antiques* (published in the U.S.A.), the *Connoisseur* and *Country Life*. Though they are specially intended for members it is possible to obtain the published *Transactions* (or lectures) of the English Ceramic Circle.

The Bell Works, Burslem.

PLATE 19 Engraving of the Works, Burslem, which were occupied by Josiah Wedgwood as the tenant of John Bourne until he moved to Etruria. At Burslem he concentrated upon the manufacture of fine earthenwares. This was the scene in 1865, showing the typical firing-kilns which were, and still are, such a feature of the Potteries landscape.

PART II

*A
Sequence
of
Photographs*

LEAD-GLAZED EARTHENWARE

Lovers of early lead-glazed earthenwares are attracted by their reticence and by a simple crudity that resulted from the potter's innate sense of form and fittingness. As we have already seen, he did his own decoration, without conscious thought, adding an incised line here, or placing a row of little modelled pads of clay there, his instinct telling him that by so doing some curve or swell might be emphasised. He had no tools but his simple wheel, and his glaze was so thick that he could add colour only by means of slip, coloured in green, brown, yellow or white.

The mediaeval potter made vessels for use, nor for ornament, but he seized the opportunity to display his artistic talent in the making of floor tiles for abbeys and churches, filling in with white or yellow clay a moulded or incised pattern in slabs of red; *encaustic* (burnt in) tiles may still be seen in many of our cathedrals and abbeys, though they have been trodden underfoot for at least 600 years.

Most of the surviving mediaeval wares are in the form of jugs, tall and slender in the thirteenth century, beautiful because of their graceful proportions, but usually devoid of decoration. The clay of which they were made was grey, buff or red, covered or partially covered with green or yellow glaze. During the fourteenth century they became bluntly pear-shaped, sturdy and broad-based, and more attention was given to decoration in the forms of impressed simple designs, incised trellis-work, and applied strips, rosettes, and representations of natural forms, notably birds and beasts, in contrasting colours of clay. The potter had learnt by this time the effective decorative use of coloured glazes in tones of green, yellow and brown, a practice which was still further developed during the ensuing 200 years, together with a greater use of contrasting colours of clay and, above all, of slip.

Early seventeenth-century slip-ware owed nothing to any foreign influence, it was basically intended for domestic use, and to modern eyes the contrast of subdued colour is most attractive. It would seem that its making took place in certain well-defined centres, among which were Wrotham in Kent, London and, inevitably, the Potteries. The Wrotham ware was made of red clay, decorated with white pipe-clay slip mellowed into buff by the glaze, in the forms of flowers and leaves; it usually had imitation stitching like that on leather bottles, and bucolic inscriptions likely to appeal to country folk. The London, or Metropolitan ware as it is called, was more severe and formal as a result of Puritan influence, both as regards decoration and inscriptions, which are pious in character. Much Staffordshire ware bears the names of members of the Toft family, and although other names are to be found upon it the collector has always referred to it as *Toft Ware*. Indeed, it is not certainly known whether the Tofts (and others) were the makers or the recipients of this ware, which is decorated with a great variety of ornament, flowers and leaves, heraldic beasts, birds, mermaids, human figures, busts and portraits, trellis-work and all kinds of line-and-dot patterning, in white on red, or alternatively in red and brown on white. Slip-ware was made well into the eighteenth century, with a greater use of impressed design, and a simplification of patterning which shews that more and more attention was being given to aesthetic appearance – to decoration as such. There was also the new technique of *feathering and combing*, in which slips of different colours were mingled together in all kinds of effects by the use of wooden combs. Fragments of this class of ware are often dug up in our gardens, and some are doubtless old, though it must be remembered that many a large, crudely-made dish decorated in this way, though apparently old, may be an example of the nineteenth-century ware made notably at Barnstaple, but also in the Potteries. The Devon potteries at Barnstaple, Bideford and Fremington made also what we call *sgraffito* ware, bearing designs either scratched into the surface or else cut more deeply through a layer of slip to reveal the contrasting colour of the clay beneath.

Among the personalities of eighteenth-century industrialism in the Potteries, Wedgwood and Thomas Whieldon (1719–1795) must have been outstanding, the first as leader in every aspect of potting, and the second as his chief technical helper. Whieldon was the man responsible above all for the perfected manufacture and use of coloured glazes derived from metallic oxides, seen to fine advantage in his wonderfully colourful tortoiseshell wares in mingled yellow-brown, purple, green, blue and grey. He used a copper green which may be seen on his cauliflower, pineapple and maize-cob shapes, tea-pots and other table wares, contrasting to clean, sparkling effect with the pale yellowish body. The same metallic glazes were used in the decoration of his Toby Jugs and of those made by his contemporary Ralph Wood senior. Whieldon's *agate ware* is extremely valuable, and was made by wedging together clays of different colours – blue, brown and white – which when sliced through or modelled gave a streaky effect.

John Astbury (1688–1743) made wares which are often confused with those made by Whieldon, so much so that the name of Astbury-Whieldon is often given to them, and particularly to figures. He was responsible for the ultimate development of the Elers *sprigging* technique – the application of stamped clay ornament to several kinds of bodies. These include wares in black, brown, red and yellow, in the forms of ovoid cream-jugs with pinched (*sparrow-beak*) lips, coffee-pots, and tea-pots usually mounted on three mask and claw feet, and with plain loop or *crabstock* handles. A feature of this early sprigged ornament is the contrast of colour between the applied motifs and the body, such as cream on red, green on yellow, yellow on black, and so forth.

It is at this point that we end the chapter, because although lead-glazed wares were of course made throughout the nineteenth century, they were products of a fully developed, mechanised industry, and as such do not fall into its scope.

PLATE 20 Slipware Jug. This dated jug has a
body of light brown clay, upon which the outline
of the design was drawn in darker brown slip, picked
out when dry with small dots of white slip.
Before this outlining and dotting was done the
shapes of the flowers, the leaves and the bird were
laid down in patches of reddish-brown clay. The
whole was then covered with a colourless lead glaze.

PLATE 21 Fremington Puzzle-jug. An early puzzle-jug, dated [4], and made at Fremington, [ne]ar Barnstaple. The *sgraffito* [dec]oration is in dark brown on a [bu]ff body, and the whole is covered [wi]th a colourless lead glaze. [Pu]zzle-jugs of this kind have been [ma]de in every kind of earthenware, [an]d were doubtless especially [po]pular in village inns—to be [cla]ssed with 'frog-mugs' as traps [for] the stranger.

PLATE 22 Lead-Glazed Earthenware. This is a most ambitious attempt by a mediaeval British potter, with its elaborate piercing and good proportions. Made of a yellow-glazed, buff-coloured clay. It is an ancestor of the well-known family of 'puzzle-jugs', and the six cups, and two spouts concealed in the handles all communicate with the hollow rim. It is just over six and a half inches high.

PLATE 23 Lead-glazed Earthenware. A
beaker-shaped cup, seven inches in height
with a plain knop handle and horizontal
and spiral ribbing. The well-shaped foot-rim,
comparatively elegant form, and restrained,
well-balanced decoration indicate a
sixteenth-century origin.

PLATE 24 Lead-glazed Earthenware.
The date of 1671 (with the initials $\frac{R}{EE}$)
inscribed in black slip on the front and
the streakily glazed, buff-coloured body
are in keeping with the generally
sophisticated, oviform shape of this massive
jug, thirteen inches in height.

PLATE 25 Lead-glazed Earthenware. A
two-handled cistern on barrel green glaze,
and dated 1707. In the absence of such a late
date an earlier origin might have been
given to this interesting piece, the
elementary decoration of which so readily
calls up a picture of the potter using his
finger-tips and, perhaps an old nail to
achieve his simple result.

PLATE 26 Lead-glazed Earthenware. It
is most unusual to find signed pieces of
pottery of such early date, for this
seven-sided lantern bears the name, *Isa
Wood*, with the date, 1712. It is, however
always difficult to decide whether the
occasional name on a piece of early
lead-glazed earthenware is that of its maker
or of the person for whom it was made.

PLATE 27 Lead-glazed Earthenware. Nests of cups of this kind,
more usually with three or four
cups, are sometimes called 'tygs'
or 'fuddling cups' and they were
probably used as flower vases. This
example is dated 1770 and upon it
is incised the inscription 'My
friend is he that love me well, but
who he is I cannot tell'.

ENGLISH DELFT

It was not until fine Chinese porcelain began to find its way in large quantities into Europe, during the seventeenth century, that Western eyes were opened to the fact that domestic wares could be highly decorative as well as useful. The actual decoration upon the Chinese pieces was wonderful enough, with its added exotic attraction, but in addition those who could appreciate beauty (and the potters who had to cater for them) were lost in admiration for their thinness and delicacy and, above all, of their translucency. It was easy enough to copy the decoration, but they could not puzzle out how a translucent body could be made – so the next best thing was to paint upon a surface which was as white as possible. This was obtained by the use of a lead glaze with tin oxide added to it, thickly applied to whatever kind of clay body was used.

Tin-glazed wares were made in Spain during the fifteenth century, (though not for the same reason), and the technique was copied in Germany and France (faïence), Italy (majolica) and Holland (delft). In England, roughly speaking, the delft-making centres of Bristol (1650), Lambeth (1665) and Liverpool (1710) were founded by potters who migrated from what is supposed to have been the parent factory at Southwark, London. It is supposed also that among the early wares made at this pioneer concern were the so-called 'Blue Dash Chargers' – obviously for display rather than for everyday use – designed to stand upon a dresser or a shelf, or to hang upon the wall. These important pieces have borders of short, thick strokes, usually in blue but also in other colours, and the bold decoration was done in green, brown, purple, blue and yellow. It had to be bold, because the powdery surface of the ware prevented any sort of delicate brushwork, and in that incisive boldness lies much of its attraction. Decoration was predominantly patriotic or pious, featuring Adam and Eve in particular, and portraits of Kings and Queens from Charles I onwards. There is a *Tulip* pattern featuring tulips or other large flowers, a pattern of whorls and circles in blue or purple, and an occasional rarity such as a magnificent charger in the London Museum decorated with a view of the Tower of London. Another very early type of ware consists of *Sack Bottles*, decorated in blue on the pure white enamel, bearing the names of wines and, sometimes, dates.

Apart from these early styles of decoration upon a quite distinctive kind of delft, general decoration followed an inevitable course. The intention was to imitate Chinese porcelain, and the designs upon it (and upon Dutch delft whose painters had copied from the same sources) were copied either in blue alone or in polychrome. Dealing first with Bristol, therefore, we find an abundance of blue painting of little merit, followed by more careful coloured decoration which included renderings of K'hang Hsi patterns in blue, green and orange, even to the characteristic flower-sprays beneath the rims of plates and dishes. Other styles feature flowering shrubs and flowers, and landscapes

E.C.   65   E complete with fences, winding rivers, pagodas and exotic trees. There is indeed a profusion of floral designs on Bristol delft, partly because so many appear on Chinese porcelain and partly because their drawing was so well suited to the sweeping delft-painter's style. The surrounding borders are also usually Chinese in style, with diapered pattern and reserved panels of conventionalised flowers, but an important class of Bristol ware features floral and foliate borders painted in white enamel upon a faintly blue-tinged surface – a style to which the name of *bianco sopra bianco* has been given. Among other distinctive Bristol wares are those decorated with trees sponged in with manganese brown, scenes of English ships and shipping, most carefully painted – perhaps to special order, and a few commemorative pieces such as those which bear representations of Lunardi's balloon ascent of 1784.

Because decoration had common sources and was in any case applied by wandering workmen, that which is found upon Liverpool and Lambeth delft is little different from that already described. On the whole, perhaps, the painting upon the London ware is inclined to be neat to the point of being stilted, and identification is sometimes possible because the tin enamel has a pinkish tint. Since there was no secret regarding the colours which could be used in delft painting the palettes used at all the English factories were more or less the same, though when imitating the 'crackproof' brown edges of Chinese plates and dishes the Liverpool decorators preferred to use india-red enamel, while those at Lambeth used yellow or brown. Two Liverpool specialities were tiles, printed in black or red by Sadler and Green, and shallow, straightsided *char pots*, crudely painted with fishes, and made to preserve the Lake District fish of that name.

The collector of delft must clearly be attracted by its decorative qualities, by the very crudity of the drawing which, when allied to brilliant, strong colour, is extremely attractive. Technically, of course, the ware has little to commend it. In an attempt to imitate porcelain its makers often strove after a delicacy and a thinness which an earthenware body could not well sustain. Furthermore, their object was defeated by the necessity to apply the tin enamel very thickly in order to hide the red clay beneath, with the result that it has chipped away at the edges in the course of time. Undeniable beauty is therefore to be associated with clumsiness and an inherent weakness, and it is plain to see why our potters strove to find something better.

PLATE 28   Adam and Eve Delft Charger. This dated charger was probably made at Bristol, and the initials indicate that it was made for presentation. The subject of the Fall was a favourite one on early delft, and it is here curiously allied to a border design which shows a Chinese influence.

PLATE 29 Delft Portrait Charger. A London or
Bristol charger of about 1680, decorated with a
portrait of James II in blue, purple and yellow. The
broad rim with its floral border is typical of chargers
bearing portraits either of Charles II or James II,
the same likeness (with the sardonically lifted eye)
being used for either king.

PLATE 30   Delft 'Tulip' Charger.   This fine
charger belongs to the 'blue dash' family, and its
bright decoration in blue, green, yellow and india-
red, and its boldly drawn, sweeping line give it a
beauty far above mere prettiness. It was made
about 1650, probably at Bristol, though similar
ones were made also at Lambeth, at a time when
tulips were popular in many forms of art.

PLATE 31   Delft Charger.   This is a Lambeth specimen, made about
1690. The arrangement of spirals in blue and purple is one of the
most satisfying of the several geometrical patterns, but very few
examples have survived. It is clear to see that the central spiral and the
rings of the border were applied by means of spinning the piece.

PLATE 32   Delft Posset-pot.   Sillabubs, caudles and sack-possets
were drunk from the spouts of vessels such as this, which was made at
Lambeth about 1700. The decoration, in blue, red and green, is a
crude derivation from Chinese design. The posset-pot, like the puzzle-
jug, is a purely British form, not made in delft until the late 1620s.

PLATE 33 Bristol Delft Tea Bowl and
Saucer. Probably owing to their fragile
nature, it is rare to find cups and saucers in
delft, since the desirable thin potting
was quite unsuited to the material. The
decoration, in blue, is in the Chinese
style—of a kind found more commonly
on contemporary English porcelains, painted
in underglaze cobalt-blue.

PLATE 34 Delft Plate. An unusually
detailed specimen, dated 1774 and inscribed
T^{E}C, which is attributed to Bristol. The
order is typically Chinese in style but the
main decoration is European, possibly
derived from some form of 'Gardeners'
Arms'—of the kind often seen on contemporary lead-glazed creamware.

PLATE 35 Liverpool Delft. A rare pear-shaped
vase with a lipped rim. It is painted in the Fazackerley
style with yellow and aubergine flowers growing
from a pierced rock; the buds are blue and red in
colour, and the leaves a dull greenish yellow.

SALT-GLAZED STONEWARE

A stoneware is an earthenware so vitrified at a high kiln temperature that it requires no glaze to render it non-porous, and it may even be partly trans-lucent. It is so hard and strong that it may be very thinly potted, and the mid-eighteenth-century imitators of Chinese porcelain, or at least those who sought to make some kind of ware that could rival it, brought its manufacture to a high state of perfection. Most of our stonewares were glazed with salt by the method already described, imparting to it the typical pitted, orange-skin surface, but not all. The Elers brothers, for example, made copies of the unglazed red stonewares introduced at Meissen by Böttger in imitation of the Chinese red ware, mostly in the form of small tea-pots, coffee-pots or jugs, lathe-turned or sprigged with Chinese motifs, which were in turn copied by Astbury and his son Thomas.

It seems that our very earliest wares of this kind were inspired by the Rhenish *Greybeards* or *Bellarmines*, with moulded bearded masks and coats-of-arms; they were supposedly made at Fulham, where the Rhenish grey stonewares, decorated crudely with flowers and leaves in cobalt blue, were also copied. At the same centre were made the familiar large tankards, dating to the early part of the second half of the eighteenth century, made of a brown or buff body, and decorated with ornament in low relief. Another early centre was Nottingham, the home of the grotesque Bear Jugs (modelled in the shape of bears) of a rich brown colour.

In marked contrast to these heavy, rather clumsy wares, John Dwight of Fulham took out a patent in 1671 for an early porcellanous, greyish-white stoneware, lightly salt-glazed, and suitable for delicate modelling. Dwight was indeed the first of a long line of ceramic sculptors, though his studies of children, classical figures and busts are so rare as to be virtually unobtainable, and seldom seen outside museums. For collectable specimens we must look rather to the white, light, beautifully potted domestic ware that was made in Staffordshire from about 1720 onwards.

The body of this first Staffordshire salt-glazed stoneware is white, and by and large every piece was moulded. For this purpose metal moulds were used for small pieces and alabaster for large ones, with the result that the sharpness of definition which is an important feature of the ware was never lost. Every piece could be potted thinly because of the strength of the body, which at the same time will always be found to be extremely light in weight. The potter naturally took full advantage of this strength and of the moulding process, sometimes allowing invention to outrun practicability, so that tea-pots for example, are often seen moulded in the forms of squirrels, houses, or even camels. The period of this kind of perfectly white, uncoloured ware can be placed roughly as between 1720 and 1740.

By the middle of the century Staffordshire salt-glazed stoneware had nearly approached the quality of porcelain in its hardness, whiteness and, occasionally, its translucency. The next step was to add colour, at first probably by scratching designs in the body which were then filled in with blue pigment in the sgraffito style already mentioned. William Littler of Longton Hall, a pioneer maker of salt-glazed ware before turning his hand to porcelain making, used blue in another way, by washing over the entire surface with his own distinctive *Littler's Blue*.

Until Wedgwood had perfected his creamware, which was about 1760, coloured salt-glaze had no rival. At best, it possibly has no rival even today, so warmly brilliant and jewel-like are its bright enamels, so thinly potted its body, and so dully shining its glaze. Painted decoration was at first in the Chinese taste, featuring garden scenes with or without carefully drawn figures and often with exquisitely patterned diaper borders. Then followed flower painting in the naturalistic style. Effective use was made of strongly brilliant ground colours, the best of which are ruby, turquoise, green and blue, either with flowers painted directly upon them or else in scrolled reserves, portraits of Royalty, or figure painting either rustic or in the idealised Watteau taste. We occasionally find all-over decoration, with or without reserves, in geometrical or scrolled style, or imitating natural figured stone. It will be understood, of course, that much salt-glaze decoration imitated that which is seen upon contemporary porcelain, but in addition there is a marked similarity with that used on cream-wares which indeed were made in the same shapes and of much the same body. The difference was in the kind of glaze, which in the case of the cream-ware was of a lead content, giving an altogether different surface, and imparting a yellowish tinge.

The strength and the quickly and cheaply applied form of glazing led to many revivals of stoneware in later years. Thus, Doultons of Lambeth made ornamental wares of heavy brown stoneware in Victorian times, bearing original incised decoration, and painted rather sombrely in brown, green, blue and fawn.

This revival of what is a most artistic kind of stoneware began about 1850, and under Sir Henry Doulton great advances were made, particularly in the use of the sgraffito technique. Thus, in addition to the traditional use of incised lines as the boundaries of different colours or of relief ornament, a skilled band of artists excelled in the incising of figures, animals, foliate and floral forms, and landscapes in a distinctive style which is always associated with the factory. It is important to know that each piece was an individual creation of which no copy was made, while in addition every fine specimen was signed with initials or monogram, which were of course accompanied by an impressed factory mark.

A list of more than twenty such specialised artists may be compiled, and the collector will quickly learn to recognise their particular styles. Outstanding among them were the Barlows. Hannah was apparently the first to be employed, in 1872, and she is noted for her representations of animals, while her sister Florence, who joined her later, did similar work but is famed also for her work in the pâte-sur-pâte style. Their brother, Arthur, specialised in foliate designs usually in the form of wreaths encircling his vases or jugs, held in position, apparently, by modelled ornamental bosses or studs. Another woman artist, Emily J. Edwards, was responsible for elaborately treated backgrounds with small stamped patterns of mixed conventional and natural forms. It is interesting to know that after a visit to a Doulton exhibit which was sent to Philadelphia in 1876, Gladstone made glowing reference to a particular specimen created by Frank A. Butler, who was deaf and dumb. This artist's training as a stained-glass painter is apparent in his massing together of floral and foliate forms, a style adopted also by Elise Simmance, who either carved or modelled her designs from the soft clay, or else incised green-painted leaves and shaded white flowers, with depressed centres.

A quite different kind of Doulton ware was the work of Mark V. Marshall, who specialised in carving wet clay into intricately ornate, often grotesque designs. His pieces were often of large size, such as jugs up to four feet in height, but on the other hand he was responsible also for the delicate modelling of glazed stoneware figures. Following in the early nineteenth-century tradition of the making of caudle-flasks, spirit flasks, busts and heads of topical significance – such as 'The William IV Reform Cordial', the 'Lord John Russell', and the likenesses of Nelson and Napoleon – artists such as John Broad, F. C. Pope, H. Simeon and L. Harradine modelled brown stoneware portrait flasks in the likenesses of statesmen, figures of Dickens characters, and many other wares which, unlike the incised work already discussed, were repeated in large numbers in plaster of Paris moulds. It is important to note that towards the end of 1897 the use of the incised line, which had the advantage of retaining colour exactly within its boundaries, was discontinued in favour of brushdrawn lines.

Another firm making stoneware of an ornamental kind was that of the Martin Brothers of Fulham, who specialised in the grotesque. Among their signed products are jugs representing notabilities in the shapes of birds, the heads forming the lids, and a wide range of distorted birds, beasts and monsters, all of them ogling, grimacing, leering or scowling. They are not to everyone's taste, but the modelling and decoration, carried out in browns and greys, leave nothing to be desired.

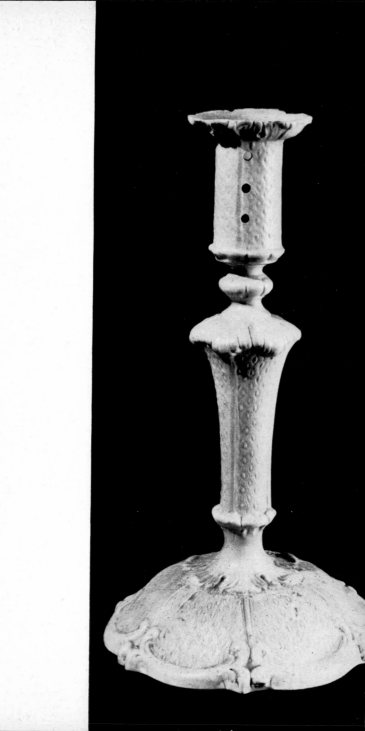

ATE 36 **Salt-glazed Candlestick.** A very lovely
imen made in Staffordshire about 1730, and
iously copied from a silver original. The detail
idence of a beautifully cut mould, which was
le in two parts, as is shown by the visible join
ch, strangely enough, was not disguised before
piece was fired.

PLATE 37 **Salt-glazed Teapot.** This illustration
shews a typical salt-glaze form, with 'crabstock'
handle and spout. The way in which the jewel-like
enamels stand out on the white body is clearly
visible, and the decoration is in Chinese style. Notice
the snugly-fitting cover, which is a feature of these
lovely teapots. It was made *circa* 1750–55.

PLATE 38 Salt-glazed Teapot.
Another type of contemporary
teapot, with the decoration, mainly
in blue, painted directly upon a
bright red ground. Notice,
however, that areas of the surface
were left white, roughly to contain
the painting, in a style not to be
confused with the provision of
clearly defined reserves.

PLATE 39   Salt-glazed Sauce-
boat. Silver-shaped boats of
this kind are found in great
variety in porcelain and earthenware of the period 1750–60. Here
is the same detailed, clear-cut
moulding which was evident in
Plate 36, allied to enamelled
decoration in almost Watteau style.

PLATE 40 Salt-glazed Plate. Apart from the monogram, this fine example incorporates low moulding in relief, pricked out in enamels, a border of flowers and diaper in Chinese style, and a contrastingly European harbour scene. The whole is painted in the glowing, vivid enamels which are the feature of the later perfected Staffordshire salt-glazed ware. It dates from about 1760, and is nine and a half inches in diameter.

PLATE 41 Staffordshire Owl Jug and
Stand.   An amusing combination of almost
primitive animal-form and careful ornamentation is accentuated by rows of dots
in brown slip, and the lid is detachable,
forming a drinking cup.

PLATE 42 Salt-glazed Cornucopia.
[W]all Pockets of this kind, usually
[in] pairs, were made in many kinds
[of] earthenware and porcelain.
[Th]is fine example, traditionally
[as]cribed to Thomas Greatback,
[be]ars a moulded cartouche of the
[g]oddess Flora. It is eleven inches
[lo]ng, and may be dated *circa* 1760.

PLATE 43 Three salt-glaze stoneware jugs. All three have carved
and relief decoration.
(*Left to right*) White, blue and dark
brown on a light slip ground;
ten and a half inches high by
George Tinworth in 1874. Light
and dark blues and white on a
buff slip ground with a dark-
brown handle; ten and a half
inches high by Arthur B. Barlow.
Light and dark blues, white and
dark-brown on a pale-green slip
ground; nine inches high by
George Tinworth, *circa* 1874.

PLATE 45 Nineteenth-century Salt-glaze. Three coloured pieces of salt-glazed Doulton stoneware. (*Left to right*) A vase with light blue slip decoration on a white body; it is eight inches high and was designed by Hannah B. Barlow in 1876. A salt-glazed stoneware jug with white slip background and incised decoration filled in with cobalt blue; eight and a half inches high designed by Hannah B. Barlow in 1875. A vase with carved decoration and light-blue and brown colouring; ten and a half inches high it was designed by Arthur B. Barlow in 1873.

PLATE 44 Stoneware Bust of Nelson. Salt-glazed stoneware, usually buff or brown in colour, was an ideal medium for the making of all kinds of ceramic statuary. There are many versions of busts of Nelson, most of them probably made in Nottingham *circa* 1825; this specimen shows very clearly the sharp detail which was made possible by the use of the salt-glaze technique. It is eight inches high.

PLATE 46   Modern White Stoneware.   A delightful figure made about 1912 by John Broad, a modeller and sculptor who was equally at home in small- and large-scale work. This piece is ten and a half inches high and is entitled 'The Bather'.

CREAM-WARE

Josiah Wedgwood (1730–1795) began business with £20 and died worth half a million. He was a man of boundless energy, courage and foresight, with great powers of organisation, and above all, a proficient businessman with a profound knowledge of ceramics. So, when as the result of a legal action between the Staffordshire potters and the Bristol porcelain makers he was prevented from making true porcelain, he lost no time, not in trying to make the artificial variety, but in perfecting a really good earthenware. He did this in the realisation that there was a great market for clean-looking, durable, cheaply made domestic ware, and basing his experiments on the successes of Whieldon, Astbury, Littler and others, by 1760 he had introduced a superior cream-ware, to which he gave the name of *Queen's Ware*.

Much of this new ware was undecorated, being indeed of such lovely design that it needed no ornament, except occasionally for pierced designs that were cut with metal dies, at first each hole separately – lozenge-shaped, irregularly curved or round – but later a whole pattern at a time with a single multiple die. Many pieces were copied from silver shapes, but he did not neglect the popular Staffordshire rustic styles of Whieldon and Astbury, with their twisted, notched or crabstock handles. Apart from pierced designs he favoured little manipulation of the clay itself, confining the use of moulding to beaded or feathered edges.

A development of Queen's Ware resulted about 1779 in the introduction of *Pearl Ware*, in which the usual creamy colour of the body was whitened by the addition of cobalt blue, but which yet has an appearance of mother-of-pearl, rather like that of Irish Belleek porcelain, when seen in a certain glancing light. Of these two bodies, in addition to everyday ware, Wedgwood made shell-like forms tinted and picked out with green or purple, tiered centre-pieces, dessert sets, complete cruets, sets of egg-cups in stands, and many kinds of decorative wares.

Although much Wedgwood cream-ware was elaborately decorated, probably outside the factory by such as Mrs. Warburton, of Hot Lane, Cobridge, it is clear that Josiah had a personal preference for simplicity, and probable that much of the rather over-decorated ware often attributed to his factory was in fact made at Leeds. Thus, we admire most, as he certainly did, the amazingly modern looking borders of husks, leaves, and formal patterning in red, black, brown or puce, so simple as to enhance the beauties of perfect line and hard, even glaze. Much ware was sent to be transfer-printed in Liverpool by Sadler and Green, at least before the factory established its own printing department about 1805. The prints, which were sometimes washed in with enamels, are often very like those which were made popular at Worcester by Hancock, including several versions of pheasant and ruins patterns.

Cream-ware

The same classical taste which inspired the Wedgwood jasper ware is evident in many of the cream-ware vases 'in the antique shape'. Some were simply ornamented with engine-turned bands, simple border forms, and gilding, but others feature applied festoons of 'drapery', or were made to imitate natural stones by the mingling of coloured clays to give what were called 'agate', 'onyx', 'pebbled', 'marbled' and 'crystalline' effects.

Wedgwood's greatest rival in the field of cream-ware was the firm of Hartley, Greens and Co. of Leeds, and it is often impossible to detect any difference between their products. Here are several pointers. Leeds ware is usually lighter, pierced work is often more clearly defined because a single tool was always used to make each aperture, flowers were often placed at handle terminals, the glaze is greenish in the angles and crevices, and whereas a Leeds plate has a low footrim, a Wedgwood one has none, being rounded beneath. The Leeds decorators made infrequent use of borders in the Wedgwood style but neglected few of the styles of decoration found upon salt-glaze – in particular flowers, ships and rustic subjects which are often accompanied by lines of doggerel verse enclosed within a frame of flowers or leaves. The colours used for enamelled decoration and for washing in extensively used black outline printing were brown, purple, black, green and red.

There is no doubt that practically every potter, in Staffordshire and elsewhere, made some kind of cream-ware, some of it marked, but much more quite unattributable. The Liverpool potteries, of which there were many, are credited with a series of large, barrel-shaped serving jugs with loop handles and sparrow-beak lips, made of a good, cream-tinted body with a blue-toned glaze. The decoration upon them usually takes the form of black-printed ships or classical subjects, but others were painted in underglaze blue in the Chinese style.

PLATE 47 Wedgwood Creamware Jug.
The black-printed decoration on this jug,
and the printed and enamelled group of
farm implements on the other side, are
typical of jugs made all over the Potteries
during the first quarter of the nineteenth
century. Apart from the presence of the
mark, *Wedgwood*, the origin of this example
would be suggested by the typically
careful laurel-leaf border.

PLATE 48 Wedgwood Vases (*Left*). A vase and cover of 'porphyry' ware with applied scroll handles and husk festoons plus traces of gilding; it is no. 7 in Josiah Wedgwood's shape book of 1770. Marked *Wedgwood and Bentley, 1772.* Its height is fourteen inches. (*Centre*) Another vase and cover of 'sprinkled porphyry' ware with a fluted body, a black-basalt plinth and traces of gilding on the swags and leaves round the neck of the vase. Marked *Wedgwood 1783.* Its height is nine and a half inches. (*Right*) A third vase and cover, this time with surface marbling, thrown and turned, applied arabesque border, traces of leaf gilding, and a reversible cover, so arranged that the vase could become a candle-holder; it has a white jasper plinth, dates from 1783 and is sixteen inches high. These vases are typical examples of Wedgwood's skill in the imitation of natural stones.

PLATE 51 Leeds Cream-War
These pieces are equally typic
of Leeds ware of the perio
Note the teapot shape with i
beaded borders and flower knob
its cover, and the gracefu
flowing contour of the coffe
pot, which is continued in th
cover. The floral decoration o
the latter specimen, of a con
ventional kind, is very like th
seen upon contemporary Ne
Hall porcelai

PLATE 49.　Leeds Creamware
...estnut Bowl, Cover, and Stand.
...auty of form is allied here to the
...nderfully delicate and accurate
...rcing which was brought to
...rfection at the Leeds factory. It
...s to be remembered that this
...rk was done when the clay was
...t, without impairing the shape,
...eemingly impossible task. There
...o need for any kind of coloured
...namentation. Note the typical
...isted borders and the flower-
...ays at the terminals. It was made
...und 1800.

▶

PLATE 50　Leeds Creamware
Mug.　Since the decoration is in
underglaze cobalt blue it was
considered proper that the normal
creamy tone of the paste should
be slightly blued.　The decoration
is a very closely copied version
of Hancocks' 'Parrot and Fruit',
which is often found on Caughly
and Worcester porcelains of the
same late eighteenth-century
date.　The mug is just under five
inches high.

PLATE 53   Wedgwood Plates. (*Left*)—
A Queen's Ware plate with a centre design
of Coverham Abbey in Coverdale.
(*Centre*)—A square compotier with a
centre design of Stoke Guilford in
Gloucestershire. Both the plate and the
compotier were trial models for the
Catherine of Russia Service, 1773. (*Right*)
—A Queen's Ware plate with a hand-
painted border in brown and blue 'wheat'
design of 1770 and taken from an original
pattern book. These pieces have in
common the typical Wedgwood use of
restrained floral borders.

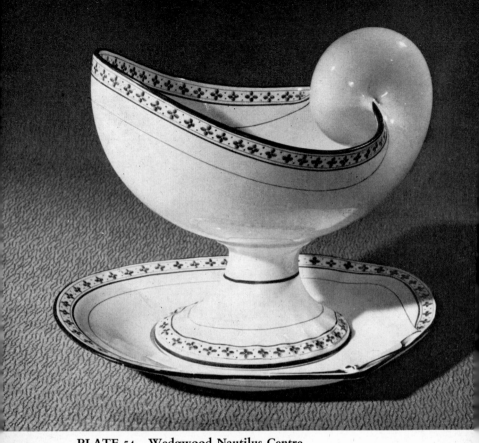

PLATE 54   Wedgwood Nautilus Centre
Piece and Stand.   From a dessert service of
the Nautilus shape in Queen's Ware. It
consists of one centre piece and stand, two
sauce tureens and stands and nine compo-
tiers. It is decorated with the No. 384 design
from Josiah Wedgwood's pattern book of
1770, and is marked *Wedgwood*. The service
was made at Etruria in 1798, and the Centre
diameter is ten inches. The service is a
very good example of Wedgwood's skill
in adopting natural forms to domestic use,
and of the effective use of a simple border.

PLATE 55 Staffordshire White Cream-
ware. The plate is a copy of early Bow
porcelain and is noteworthy for its
sharply detailed moulding. The ornament
in relief consists of six sprigs of prunus.
The diameter measures eight and three
quarter inches, and the piece was made
around 1756.

PLATE 56 Staffordshire White Creamware.
This chestnut-bowl, cover and stand is of
a form found also in early-English porcelain
work at Bow, Derby and Worcester.
Common to all are the piercing, the flower-
heads rendered in low relief, the twisted
'rope' handles, and the applied flowers at
the handle terminals. This piece is marked
John Daniel 1775, and is five and three
quarter inches high.

PLATE 57   Leeds Creamware Basket.
At the time when this piece was made, about
1780, the 'exotic bird', here printed in
black overglaze, was a favourite decoration
on English earthenwares and porcelains. The
actual basket form is a rather simplified
version of similar pieces made notably at
Worcester and to a lesser extent at Derby.

PLATE 58 Staffordshire Creamware Plates.
There was a ready sale for pieces bearing
portraits of notabilities during the first
half of the nineteenth century, and this
plate is a typical example of the
economical use of printed decoration,
cheaply and quickly applied, and of
restrained, painted borders in the cream-
ware style perfected by Wedgwood.

THE WEDGWOOD SCHOOL

Many who have not held the high opinion of Josiah Wedgwood which I expressed in the previous chapter have accused him of being, among other things, a mere copier of the antique and the classical. An obvious answer to this accusation is that he copied nothing that was not beautiful and worthwhile. Furthermore, the wares he made, in whatever style or material, were so copied by his contemporaries that in the absence of marks it can often only be said that they are 'of the Wedgwood school'.

We have already seen that the fashion for cream-ware was set by Josiah, and similarly in the quite different class of purely ornamental wares he was responsible for the introduction and popularity of the *jasper* body. This was a very hard, semi-translucent, finely-grained stoneware, the intense whiteness of which could be stained with the usual metallic oxides to produce yellow, black, lilac, olive or sage green, and light or dark blue. This was perfected about 1775, and about two years later a variant called *jasper-dip* was introduced, in which only the surface of the ware was coloured.

The jasper body, in either form, was extremely suited to imitating the classical shapes and styles of ornamentation, particularly with regard to decoration in low relief. Jasper ware is more often found in two colours, with delicately stamped, applied white reliefs on the coloured ground, though three or even more colours were sometimes used on one object. The reliefs (which though usually white could of course be of any colour) were most carefully moulded, and finished by trimming and undercutting, and since the white paste could be made transparent at will, the colour of the body beneath often shows through at the edges, giving a most light and delicate effect.

Together with his colleague Thomas Bentley, Wedgwood sought untiringly for suitable classical models worthy of the skill of a band of artists and designers which included William Hackwood, John Flaxman, James Tassie and George Stubbs. A very wide range of sets of small cameos of famous men, plaques for insertion in furniture and fireplaces, sets of chessmen, chandeliers, ornamental vases and domestic wares was produced, of a beauty and technical excellence which reached its peak in the production of the famous copy of the ancient glass Portland Vase, reproduced (and repeated and imitated many times since) in blue-black and white jasper.

The black version of jasper should not be confused with Wedgwood's *black basalt* body, which, made from a different formula, was an improvement upon the Elers black. It is indeed difficult to distinguish between the two, but whereas the jasper black was used in conjunction with white reliefs, the black basalt was usually reserved for all-black domestic services and for busts and statuettes, for which its dull sheen and subdued high-lights were admirably suitable. Added ornament on domestic wares and ornamental pieces was sometimes used in the forms of coloured enamels or low reliefs in red, and a wonderful imitation of bronze could be obtained by mixing powdered metal with the body materials. Another Wedgwood improvement on an Elers body was his red *rosso antico*, often decorated with flowers in rather flat enamels. His *terra cotta* range is best known for its cane-coloured wares, but it also included others in green or chocolate, and most effective combinations of all three. We should not forget in selecting from a range of wares, too extensive to describe fully, the Wedgwood imitations of natural stones that were mentioned in the previous chapter.

Josiah set the fashion, and every potter of note imitated the styles which proved to be popular. His jasper, in particular, was equalled if not excelled by William Adams of Greengates who, though his blue was perhaps a little too violet and his green rather yellowish, produced reliefs remarkable for their design and delicacy. Adams is also known to collectors as a maker of fine cream-ware and black basalt, stoneware jugs and mugs decorated with sporting and drinking subjects in low relief, and blue-printed earthenware, though it was his namesake, Adams of Cobridge, who really perfected the process, helped by William Davis of the Worcester porcelain factory.

John Turner was a maker of fine jaspers, working at Lane End from about 1762, but he is especially known for his white stoneware and black basalt. A typical Turner stoneware jug is decorated with hunting scenes in clear-cut low relief, it has a band of strong blue enamel round the rim, and it may be mounted with silver or Sheffield Plate. His cream-ware is markedly yellow in tone, and the presence upon many pieces of biblical scenes with Dutch inscriptions suggests that they were painted by outside Dutch decorators who had settled in the Potteries, having originally come into the country to paint delft.

It is perhaps necessary again to stress the fact that literally hundreds of factories were working in Staffordshire during Wedgwood's lifetime, all making exactly the same kinds of ware, and in the absence of marks the only clue to provenance is provided by exceptional quality or by some distinctive style that for some reason or other was not copied by others. Thus, Samuel Hollins made a series of quite distinctive tea-pots, coffee-pots and mugs in chocolate or red stoneware, decorated in low relief and banded with silver or gun-metal toned lustre. At the opposite extreme, it seems that no single potter neglected to make some kind of earthenware printed in underglaze blue. Some pieces are marked, but otherwise quality is so uniformly high that identification is possible only by a study of border designs or by the recognition of some particular pattern.

PLATE 59 Three Jasper Medallions by
Wedgwood. On the left is 'Venus and
Cupid', attributed to William Hackwood,
in a gilt frame, dating from *circa* 1778. It
is five and a half inches high. The middle
medallion, 'The Choice of Hercules',
was modelled by Hackwood in about
1777. It is in an ormulu frame and is
thirteen inches long. 'Erato' is the
name of the medallion on the right and it
also is attributed to Hackwood. This has a
gilt frame and is five and a half inches high.
Circa 1778. All three medallions are
white on blue.

lt.   One of a pair of seated
ins in black basalt which
ort brass candleholders; they
oblong rectangular bases and
and dart border. The mark is
wood. They were made at
ria in about 1785. The height
velve and three quarter inches.
dense black body was brought
erfection by Wedgwood, and
admirably suitable for ceramic
pture. The illustration shows
rly the fine detail into which
ould be modelled.

PLATE 61   The First Day's Vase.
On June 13th in 1769 Josiah
Wedgwood, F.R.S. and his
partner, Bentley, moved from
the old Bell Works to their new
factory, Etruria. On that day six
Black Basalt vases were made to
commemorate the event. While
Bentley turned the wheel Josiah
'threw' the vases which were then
painted with red classical figures
in Etruscan style. Each was
inscribed *Artes Etruriae Renascuntur*—
'The arts of Etruria are re-born'.

PLATE 62   Wedgwood Antique
Black Basalt.   A cup and saucer
in black basalt, decorated in
red and white encaustic colours.
The set was made in 1778, and is
two and a half inches in height. The
teapot is in black basalt, thrown
and engine-turned; it has a lion
knob and a top cup in the form of
a low parapet. It was made in 1780
and is four and a half inches high.

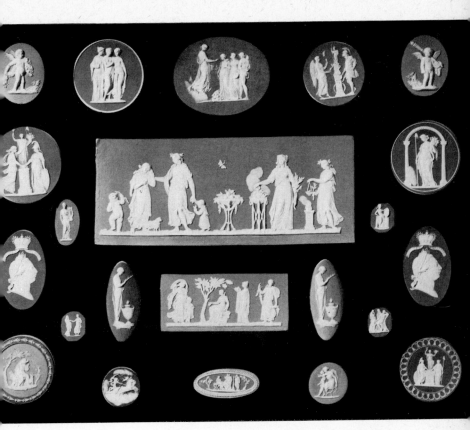

PLATE 63   Wedgwood Jasper
Medallions.   A frame of twenty-
two Jasper medallions and
plaques with 'Sacrifice to Peace' in
the centre. They were made at
Etruria around 1775–1790. There
are many ways of displaying these
lovely medallions and plaques,
regardless of the purposes for
which they were originally made.
Here is an ideal arrangement.

PLATE 64 Wedgwood Early
Morning Tea-set. There are five
pieces—teapot with a cover, sugar
box with cover, cream jug, cup and
saucer, and tray. It is made in white
on blue jasper and thrown and
engine-turned. The reliefs by Lady
Templetown are of 'Domestic Em-
ployment, and (on the teapot) 'Poor
Maria'. The pieces date from 1784,
and the tea-pot is four inches high.

PLATE 65 Wedgwood Pai
'Rustic' Candlesticks. 'Summ
and 'Winter', modelled
William Hackwood in jasper;
colours are white on sage gr
They date from 1784, and
ten inches in height. The cont
of applied white ornamentat
on a coloured jasper groun
here allied to good modell
and well-balanced desi

PLATE 66 Wedgwood Jasper Wares.
The centrepiece is blue jasper with applied
yellow and white strapwork, applied
flowers inside the bowl, and a scroll and rope
border to foot. It dates from 1790, and is
nine and a half inches in diameter. The
oblong dish is white jasper with blue,
yellow and white strapwork. It also dates
from 1740 and is seven and a half inches long.
Both these pieces illustrate an interesting
and effective use of the jasper body.

PLATE 67 Turner Stoneware Ju
John Turner and his sons John and Willia
were outstanding rivals to Wedgwo
from about 1755 to 1803. This particul
example, marked *TURNER*, impresse
was made about 1790–1800, and is typic
of Turner stoneware jugs as regar
shape, the brown-glazed neck (oft
fitted with silver mounts), and the sharp
moulded hunting-scene and vine bord

Engraved by W.Holl.

JOSIAH WEDGWOOD.

PLATE 69 Blue-printed Staffordshire Dish. By the time that this dish was made by John Meir & Son of Tunstall, about 1825-30, the process of printing in underglaze blue had been perfected, and was extensively used by practically every Staffordshire potter. Here is a purely British style of decoration, with a border of roses. In the absence of marks much of this ware can be identified by means of border patterns of which there is a very great variety.

H 2

PLATE 70   Copeland (Late Spode) Dish.
A late nineteenth-century example of the
perfected Spode blue-painting by Charles
Ferdinand Hürten. This proficient artist
was engaged by Messrs. Copeland in 1858,
his work at the International Exhibition in
Paris having attracted their admiration;
he worked for the firm for nearly forty
years.

MISCELLANEOUS EARTHENWARES

The previous chapters have dealt with wares that fall into definable classes, but it must be obvious that certain hybrid earthenwares or stonewares, and indeed certain styles of decoration do not fall conveniently within their scope. Furthermore, the nature of the classification which I have used has meant that the work of quite a number of world-famous factories has been neglected.

No factory, perhaps, is more famous than Spode, with which the name of Copeland is almost synonymous. If we except delft, the Spodes, father and son, made every conceivable kind of ware superlatively well and neglected no styles of decoration, though if one had to choose from their many triumphs mention should be made of their wonderfully strong *Stone China*, an earthenware which was introduced in 1805, and of their perfecting of the process of outline printing, used as the foundation for wide ranges of ground colour, patterning, enamel washing and gilding – in other words, many different treatments of any single outlined design.

It was natural that others should strive to emulate the Spode success in making a strong, white earthenware body suitable for hard, everyday use. Among those whose wares are good enough to interest the collector were Davenports of Longport (very good willow pattern and simple conventional designs in red, blue and green), Minton (well-known for their *Amherst Japan* series), Johnson, Meigh, Allerton (simple-decoration combinations of blue bands, india-red and green flower-sprigs and purple lustre). Alcock and Hicks. All these and others made the same kind of serviceable ware, and many of the names given to their bodies include the meaningless word, 'Ironstone', among them being *Mason's Patent Ironstone China*. This rather remarkable ware was the product of C. J. Mason & Co. from 1813 until 1851, when Ashworths took it over to use the same mark on the same kind of ware up to the present day. The intention was to provide the poor man's substitute for splendid Chinese porcelain, and though some good landscape and flower painting was done the decoration was for the most part outline printed and washed in with enamels. Decoration ran the gamut of every Oriental style of the more splendid kind, and specialities included complete fireplace-surrounds, enormous vases with encrusted flowers and handles and knobs shaped like dragons or kylins, exceptionally large dinner services and, of course, the typical Mason's octagonal jugs with snake handles, made in many sizes.

Just as Mason's Ironstone China was the poor man's Oriental, so was *lustre* his silver and gold. The familiar lustred appearance was given to ordinary red earthenware or to cream-ware by means of metallic salts, platinum for silver, gold for pink or purple, and copper for gold, bronze or copper. All kinds of painted decoration were applied over the lustre, or painted or printed in reserves or in reserved bands. The process was probably first used by Wedgwood, but during the first quarter of the nineteenth century manufacture had spread to Swansea, Leeds, Bristol, Sunderland and, of course, throughout the Potteries. In the absence of marks it is difficult to identify ordinary specimens, but Sunderland is credited with the making of large jugs, bowls and mugs bearing printed representations of the famous Wear Bridge, masonic emblems, ships and hunting scenes, with or without verses, and of rectangular wall-plaques bearing religious texts, ships or mariners' compasses, always accompanied by purple or pink lustre. We have already mentioned the most beautiful and expensive kind of lustre, the *silver resist*, on white, yellowed or blued body, with or without the addition of enamelled decoration.

Pratts of Fenton, inventors of the first successful colour-printing process, applied it to the decoration of pot-lids and to fine dessert services, and the same firm specialised between about 1780 and 1820 in jugs, tea-pots, flasks and plaques moulded in low relief with busts of famous admirals and generals, and sentimental or sporting subjects, often with acanthus-leaf ornament at rims or bases, and painted with strong, fresh, high-temperature enamels in green, red, blue, and muddy yellow.

There have been many imitations of the famous Rockingham manganese brown glaze of the period about 1796 to 1806, found chiefly upon frog-mugs, Toby jugs, flasks in the forms of pistols or boots, and Cadogan tea-pots in the shape of peaches, copied from the Chinese wine-pot, and filled through a hole in the bottom so as to be un-spillable.

Many porcelain-making factories made earthenware before rising to better things, among them the Salopian Caughley concern, situated in the Severn valley near Ironbridge. Until Thomas Turner took over to make porcelain between 1772 and 1775, earthenware had been made under the proprietorship of a Mr. Gallimore, at least as early as 1754, and the wares usually credited to him do in fact bear a family likeness to the later porcelain. We find the typical tall, narrow coffee-cup with a high foot-rim, rectangular in section, and a plain loop handle. The glaze is brilliant, rather blued, and often crazed, and the decoration, painted or printed in underglaze blue, is usually in some form of willow-pattern style, with intricate, closely drawn diaper borders and, sometimes, bands of gilding at rim and base. At nearby Broseley clay pipes were made from time immemorial, and Jackfield, a stone's throw distant, is known for its lustrous, black-glazed wares, made from local red clay, produced between 1760 and 1765 under the ownership of Maurice Thursfield. Some pieces, mostly tea-pots, jugs and bowls bear applied ornament in the Astbury style, mostly in the form of vine leaves, while others are crudely enamelled with bouquets of flowers, with here and there a mere trace of the unfired size-gilding that once lightened the appearance of what is otherwise a rather uninteresting ware.

PLATE 71 Spode Earthenware Plate. A
typical example of the early nineteenth-
century Spode use of a printed outline
(in this case in blue) which was washed in
with overglaze enamels, a process which
relieved the painter from routine and
prevented deterioration of pattern as a
result of continual copying. The name
given to this design, clearly of Chinese
origin, was 'Tumbledown Dick'. In this
original form with a white background
it is most attractive, and it was followed
by variations with yellow and other
backgrounds, which had patterning in
'cracked-ice' network.

ATE 72   Mason's Patent Ironstone China Vase.
h large vases as this, over three feet in height,
esent the kind of important pieces that were
le by Mason during the first half of the nineteenth
ury. They made an admirable, comparatively
ip substitute for the kind of Chinese porcelain
  was coveted by the rich Midlands industrialist.

PLATE 73   Lead-glazed Earthenware.   A teapot
and lid made in Staffordshire *circa* 1740. It is one
of the large number of pieces, made around the
middle of the eighteenth century, in the Astbury
style. It is five and three eighth inches high and four
and a half in diameter.

PLATE 74   Silver-resist Lustre Jug.   This
jug may be dated about 1810, and is typical
of the plainer kind of silver-resist, with no
added colour. The white areas would have
been masked from the lustering solution
by brushed-on adhesive, possibly sugar and
glycerine, which could be washed off in
warm water together with its superimposed
layer of lustre. The outlines of the leaves,
and the tendrils, would be drawn separately
with a brush.

PLATE 75 Pratt Moulded Jug. During the first half of the nineteenth century every factory had its own distinctive type of production, even though commercial pirating was the order of the day. This kind of jug, moulded in low relief and painted with high-temperature enamels in blue, green and yellow, is typical of those made by Felix Pratt of Fenton. Many are of this commemorative type, featuring personalities of the times; others feature sporting, rustic and sentimental subjects.

PLATE 76 Mason's Ironstone China. A pair of
lidded vases and a hexagonal jug of typical shape,
printed and washed in with enamels, with Chinese
landscapes reserved on a royal blue ground. Whereas
the patterning on the vases is in gold, that upon
the jug is in yellow enamel—a cheaper substitute
which was often used. These pieces may be dated
circa 1830–40.

PLATE 77 Broseley Clay Pipes. The ma
of clay pipes is an interesting branch of r
ceramics, and Broseley was a centre of it for
centuries. The making of pipes with stems six
to eighteen inches in length was perfecte
Noah Reden early in the nineteenth century,
to his mid-nineteenth century descendants
be credited the introduction of 'churchwardens'
'London Straws'. In 1860 the then proprietor o
works, a Mr. Southorn, introduced tra
painting on pipes, and the use of initials, monogr.
and even armorial bearing upon pipes ord
by clubs, societies, inns and pat

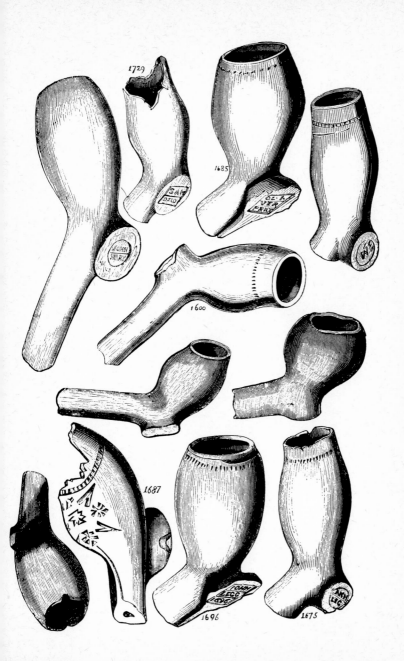

PLATE 78 Rockingham 'Cadogan' Teapot.
These amusing pots, copied from a well-
known shape of Chinese wine-pot in the
form of a peach, were made to be filled
from a hole in the base—on the principle
of an unspillable inkwell. They were
probably named after the Earl of Cadogan,
and were introduced at Rockingham in
brown-glazed form, about 1806. Similar
pots were made by Spodes, and always
marked. Mintons also produced a model
about 1877.

EARTHENWARE FIGURES

One of the greatest attractions of earthenware figures made between about 1725 and 1850 is that they represent a purely British art that seldom owed anything to outside foreign influence. The more sophisticated, more carefully modelled ceramic sculptures of Bow, Chelsea and Derby were made for those who were already familiar with originals made on the continent, and who demanded cheaper and more easily obtained substitutes, but their earthenware poor relations were intended for the mantelpieces of cottages and country inns, they were hawked from door to door by the pedlars, or sold at the country fair for a few pence apiece. And since they were designed to appeal to rustic taste their subjects were such as would appeal to the countryman, featuring animals, sportsmen and so on, sometimes crudely and even cruelly humorous, often sentimental, but always colourful. True, their makers did occasionally fall into the traps of imitating porcelain models or of copying the classical, but even then their work attracts by its simplicity, its straightforward modelling, and its subdued but often glowing colour.

The earliest figures were made of salt-glazed stoneware, they date from about 1730, and they are so rare that they are seldom seen outside museums and in famous collections. They take the form of small animals and human figures, but the potter occasionally excelled himself by producing such tours-de-force as the famous *Bell Woman* and *Pew Group*. The plain white body was sometimes lightly decorated with touches of black, blue or manganese brown, eyes are blobs of dark clay, and the limbs are like pipe-stems, with no joints to speak of. Equally rare are the *agate ware* animals, mostly cats, which have already been mentioned.

Between about 1740 and 1750 lead-glazed earthenware figures were made in Staffordshire by many potters, whose anonymity is usually represented by John Astbury and Thomas Whieldon. By and large an Astbury figure is expected to feature the use of brown or cream clays, covered with a clear glaze, and of blobs for the characteristic beady eyes, features that are seen to perfection in the sets of musicians (on foot or mounted) which are credited to this potter. Whieldon, on the other hand, made a wider range of figures which all feature the prolific use of his remarkable coloured glazes. The problem is that many figures of the period combine the characteristics of the work of both men, and the use of the term, 'Astbury-Whieldon' is a conveniently wise solution.

Ralph Wood (1715–1772) carried on the Whieldon coloured-glaze tradition in his production (helped by his nephew Enoch) of much better modelled, carefully detailed figures in a wide range of styles. A list of upwards of a hundred and sixty recorded models includes sporting types, religious subjects, sentimental ones, famous people, and classical figures many of which were designed by a French modeller named John Voyez, a former Wedgwood employee. Among notable Ralph Wood models are several groups, including the *Vicar and Moses, Parson and Clerk* and *St George and the Dragon*, and there is a wide range of Toby Jugs, all coloured, on a cream-ware body, with glazes in green, greyish-blue, brown, grey, yellow and aubergine. Many of Wood's figures and groups are to be found 'in the white', though for the most part they feature the use of the same coloured glazes. The younger Ralph Wood carried on making the same models, but used more and more enamels instead of coloured glazes, thus entirely losing the old, mellow beauty which is the greatest attraction of Ralph Wood pottery. Enoch Wood, whose *John Wesley* is probably best known, continued the Wood tradition before and after he was joined by James Caldwell in 1790, but repetition led to loss of vitality, and to a stiffness for which no amount of careful enamelling could compensate.

The period between about 1790 and 1820 covers the work of a host of potters who catered for rustic taste. Pratt figures are crude, modelled with little attention to detail, and decorated with the same distinctive enamels which were mentioned in the previous chapter. John Walton of Burslem was the leader of a school of Staffordshire figure makers which included Obadiah Sherratt, Charles Tittensor, Ralph Hall and Ralph Salt, and his groups and figures, all in patriotic, sentimental, pious or sporting mood, are characterised by the presence of crude *bocage* in the porcelain style, and are often marked with the name impressed, as are many Salt specimens. Sherratt was responsible for many very ambitious groups, mounted upon four or six-legged slab bases or platforms, such as the many versions of bull-baiting, and to the Tittensors are credited rather small bocage figures featuring a pair of cherubs standing one on either side of an urn. Neale and Palmer figures, many of them in classical style, are mounted upon plain or moulded square bases bearing a line of purple, pink or red. They are usually quite delicately modelled ('chaste, dignified and decorous' is an apt description), and some attempt at elaboration in the porcelain style is seen in the form of sprigged or dotted costume.

The largest and perhaps most inferior class of Staffordshire figures embraces a very large number of Victorian 'Chimney Ornaments', which were moulded, with no attempt at modelling, and which were clearly intended to stand upon a chimney-piece. They are indeed for the most part flat-backed, for there was no need to shape or to decorate parts which were not meant to be seen. Many are of large size, up to over a foot in height, and the range of subjects is almost endless. In fact, their makers were so quick to seize upon any topical event that might be a suitable subject, that their products might almost be said to follow the broadsheet and to anticipate the modern newspaper. Crime, politics, religion, everything and everybody that were in the public eye at any particular time, made acceptable subjects. Often the same mould was used for several different subjects, with an alteration of course in the painted or gilt title or with no title at all, for most bear no inscription. Decoration was

Earthenware Figures

carried out in strong green, red, pink and blue, with bright gilding. Of the smaller models we admire most the small dogs, deer, cows, sheep and other animals, some quite well-modelled and decorated, reclining or standing on blue bases. This was the period also of the cruder one-piece form of pastille burners, money-boxes, or romantic castles, cottages and churches. It is interesting to realise that even at this late date there lingered a trace of the early Chinese influence in the form of the descendants of the Chinese Dogs of Fo who keep ceaseless guard at a temple gate. In other words, the typical Staffordshire dog, large or small, with a golden chain around his neck, was made to stand on either side of a cottage fireplace or upon the mantelpiece, as the guardian of the home. Some are plain, others are spotted, sprigged or lustered, and all have the same docile, vacant expression.

PLATE 79 Various Staffordshire Figures.   This is a fairly representative group of early figures in various styles. Those on the top row, left to right, are by: Ralph Wood senior, Whieldon, Whieldon, Ralph Wood Senior; and on the bottom row: Ralph Wood Senior, Astbury-Whieldon, Astbury-Whieldon, Astbury-Whieldon and Ralph Wood Senior.

80a

PLATE 81 Ralph Wood Fi
of Jupiter. A 'Jupiter with Ea
ten and a half inches hig
given the mould number
in a compiled list of kn
marked, Ralph Wood fig
This particular example
this number, and is deco
with coloured glazes. It
from about

80b

PLATES 80a and 80b Astbury-
Whieldon Figures. These are
typical figures of the period
circa 1745, one in the classical
style, the other a seated musician,
both decorated with coloured
glazes. The illustration shews
clearly the characteristics of this
kind of ware—the simple modelling, the lustrous, shimmering
glaze, and the blobbed eyes. It
is interesting to know that both
were bought, some thirty years
ago, from a tray labelled 'All at
7/6'.

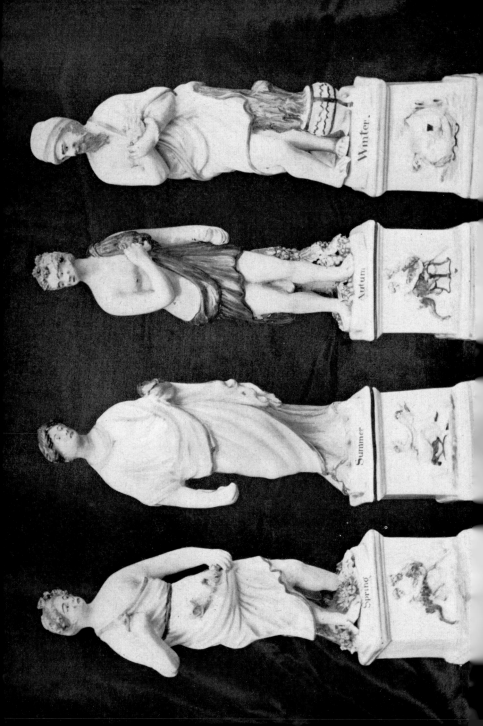

PLATE 83 Pratt 'Umbrella Courtship' Group. The 'Umbrella Courtship' was a subject favoured by many potters, and this example, made about 1790–1800, is attributed to Felix Pratt of Fenton, since it is decorated with the same distinctive enamels that are to be seen upon his moulded jugs. The modelling is admittedly crude, but the piece is attractive, and likely to have appealed to the sentimental countryfolk for whom this kind of ware was made.

A very rare set which represents the Staffordshire potter's attempt to interpret the classical style to which his medium was not really suited. An interesting feature is the set of charming little low reliefs upon the bases, picked out in colour. The set is attributed to Enoch Wood, of the period *circa* 1790.

PLATE 84 Milking Scene Group. An elaborate group, made as a flower-holder, and shewing the crudely modelled bocage that is typical of the figures and groups made by John Walton between 1780 and 1840. The decoration is enamelled, for coloured glazes had by that time been discarded in favour of the cheaper, more easily applied brushwork.

PLATE 85 Ralph Wood Toby Jug. The illustration does not show the mellow beauty of the typical coloured glazes, but the superior modelling of this 'Thin Man' model suffices to distinguish it from later versions that were made of most of the Ralph Wood models well into the first half of the nineteenth century.

PLATE 86 Obediah Sherratt Group. Obediah Sherratt (Sharratt or Skerratt) was born about 1775 and worked from about 1808 in Hot Lane, Burslem. He is famed as the maker of 'Bull Baiting' groups and of elaborate pieces such as this, mounted upon slab bases with high feet. 'Polito's Menagerie', as it is called, was one of his earlier productions, produced probably about 1814, and it is known that the menagerie visited Wolverhampton in 1808. It should be noted that the same model was later copied by other Staffordshire potters—with suitable alterations—and indeed after Sherratt's death it appeared with the new name of 'Wombwell's Circus'.

PLATE 87 Staffordshire Dovecote Ornament. A most unusual
'mantelpiece ornament', dating from about 1770–1790, thirteen inches
in height, and painted in enamels. Notice the drawer below, and the
paw feet in the contemporary furniture style.

PLATE 88 Staffordshire Group. This
late eighteenth-century group is typically
crude, but the modelling of the horse is
unusually spirited. It typifies the rustic
humour of the time, and such an accident,
perhaps a little exaggerated, would be
perfectly familiar to the countryfolk for
whom the model was intended.

BOW PORCELAIN

When the Bow porcelain-making factory was founded about 1744 by Thomas Frye and Edward Heylyn the intention was to make a durable, sensibly decorated domestic ware, and not to try to rival the splendours of the ware made at neighbouring Chelsea, apart from an occasional colourfully painted service, and for figures which had to be made to meet an overwhelming demand.

From the beginning until about 1749 the artificial paste which the proprietors had evolved was little more than a glass, containing pipeclay to give it whiteness, but from that time onwards until the closure in 1776 a bone-ash content was added to give strength, though the alteration resulted in a marked opacity which is a feature of much Bow ware. In fact, when I first began to collect *blue and white* porcelain I well remember rejecting what I later knew to be a pair of lovely Bow leaf dishes, simply because their complete opacity persuaded me that they were made of earthenware. The glaze on the early wares was also very glassy and milky in appearance – and slightly opaque because it also had a pipe-clay content – but the glaze which was made to cover the bone-ash paste was of the lead type, shewing greenish blue in the crevices and sometimes discolouring to shew brown patches.

Among the earliest wares of the pre-1755 period were copies of white Chinese blanc-de-chine – of the kind that had been extensively copied also at Meissen, St Cloud and Chantilly, decorated with sprigged ornament in the form of hawthorn or prunus, and occasionally painted as well with flower-sprays, though by far the greater part of the output was painted in underglaze cobalt-blue. It was inevitable, of course, that the same patterns, being copies of the Oriental, should be found in this medium on all contemporary early porcelains, but the Bow blue, either very pale or very dark, is quite distinctive, and certain patterns and styles are characteristic. The Bow artists loved the peony, allied usually to certain simple cell-diaper borders which should be examined and memorised. Octagonal plates and dishes are common, decorated in powder-blue like those made at Worcester and Lowestoft, but marked differently and shewing the typical greenish glaze inside the angle of the foot-rim. Powder-blue vine-leaves and grapes on a white ground are peculiar to Bow, and no other factory made such a wide use of Buddhistic religious symbols. Patterns which were apparently not copied by other factories include the *Image* and *Lady playing on a Koto*, but the so-called *Jumping Boy* was a favourite also at Liverpool. Blue printing was not practised at Bow to any important extent.

Any moulded shape is easy to copy, but certain Bow shapes and peculiarities of shape are characteristic. The Bow mug is much wider at the base than at the rim, and its handle commonly has a heart-shaped lower terminal. Sparrow-beak cream-jugs do not often bell out at the rim, but have a truncated appearance.

Bow Porcelain

Little blue painting was done after about 1755, probably because Worcester had captured the market with its blue-printing, and the polychrome decoration which was placed upon the wares falls into two well-defined classes. The first comprises imitations of the Chinese *famille-rose* porcelains, carried out in a palette of pink, pale green, pale opaque blue and aubergine (a peculiar purplish-mauve colour). Most of the patterns are floral, and the style, being peculiar to Bow, is very easily recognised. The second style comprises copies of the *Japan*, *Imari* or *Kakiemon* designs, gracefully drawn, well and reticently spaced, in clear enamels which include a good 'sealing-wax' red. The nicknames given to some of these designs have been mentioned in a previous chapter.

In 1756 some of the artists from Chelsea, then nearing closure, migrated to Bow, but they do not appear to have had a very great influence on decorative policy. True, ground colours were occasionally used, a touch or two of gilding, and some rare representations of Watteau-like subjects, but otherwise we see little change.

The very early Bow figures were extremely crude, clumsily modelled, and marred by firing defects. They, and later figures, are heavy for their size, thick-walled because they were made by pressing the paste into moulds, and not by the slip casting methods used at Chelsea. About 1754, however, perhaps partly as a result of the engagement of new workmen and partly because of the improvement in the paste, modelling became neater, poses more spontaneous, and colours were introduced in the typical Bow palette of opaque light-blue, yellow, emerald green and deep crimson. Bases, at first plain or decorated with flowers and leaves in low relief, were now painted with scrolls in purple-black or crimson, and still later the scrolls were actually modelled in relief, and picked out in crimson.

Just as at Chelsea the reticence of the earlier period was followed by comparative garishness, so the Bow modellers of the period from about 1759 to 1763 strove after more lavish effects by the introduction of the typical rococo base, raised on S-shaped feet with a pierced *apron* falling between them, by more copious application of colour, and by the occasional use of bocage. This was a style which continued to the end, though paste and quality of colour deteriorated to an extent which was not compensated for by an increased use of gilding, or by ormolu mounts which were intended to fit into the square holes which are so often found at the back of Bow figures.

PLATE 89 Bow Sauce-boat. The peony was a popular motif in Bow decoration which on this piece is in pale underglaze blue in the Chinese style. The shape was copied from a silver model, and although the size is large (nine inches long) it is extremely heavy even for its size, being very thickly potted with hardly any translucency. A similar sauce-boat in the Victoria and Albert Museum bears an incised planet mark. Both would date from the 1750–55 period.

PLATE 90 Bow Plate. The ground is white with yellow and puce exotic birds in the midst of green foliage. Blue insects and butterflies decorate the rim. The width of the plate is eight inches, and it dates from around 1756.

PLATE 91 Bow Mongolians. A fine
pair of Bow white busts of Mongolians,
their heads turned. The man has a pointed
hat, moustache and beard, ruff and
a braided coat; his companion has her hair
dressed and is wearing a necklace. They
stand on waved and spreading socles. Made
about 1750 they are over ten inches high.

PLATE 92 Bow Plate. Decoration of this
ambitious kind is rarely found on Bow porcelain,
even on that of the late period around 1770, which
is assigned to this specimen. The idyllic scene in
Watteau style is carefully painted in brilliant
enamels, and the moulded edge and deep *gros-bleu*
border are gilded. The mark is the anchor and
dagger in red.

PLATE 93 Bow Pair of Vases. These finely shaped
vases may date from the period 1750–60, and are
good examples of underglaze-blue decoration in
the prevailing Chinese style. The presence of some
of the 'Eight Precious Objects' (*pa pao*) around the
bases is a typical Bow feature.

PLATE 95 Bow Inkwell. It is supposed that these
rare inkwells were made to celebrate the opening
of the new factory at Stratford-le-Bow, which was
called 'New Canton'. This particular, dated
example is decorated in enamels of the *famille verte*,
but others were painted in underglaze blue.

...ATE 94 Bow White Figure. This figure of
...y Clive was made in 1750, since that date is
...sed beneath the base. The actress is depicted in
...role of the 'Fine Lady' in Garrick's farce, *Lethe*,
...is modelled after an engraving by Charles
...ley. It was made as a companion to Henry
...odward, in the character of the 'Fine Gentleman'.
...figure is twelve and a half inches high.

PLATE 96 Bow Set of the Four Seasons.
A set of figures, six and a half inches in
height, with typical rococo-scrolled bases,
enamelled predominantly in puce, blue and
yellow, and gilded. Sets of Seasons were
made in many styles at many of the early
English factories, and though unmarked
this set may be dated about 1756.

PLATE 97 Bow Porcelain Clock. Clock-cases of this kind, of rococo form, are commoner in Continental than in English porcelain. This specimen, which stands thirteen inches in height, belongs to the period around 1757.

PLATE 98 Bow Pair of Monkeys. An
extremely rare if not unique pair of figures,
dressed in yellow and puce, dating from the
period 1757–58. The scrolled bases are
typical, the modelling of high quality, and
the enamelling restrained.

CHELSEA PORCELAIN

The magic name of Chelsea is associated for most of us with elegance, with dainty, expensively decorated porcelain which was made for the fashionable London world of Society at a time when the wares of Meissen and Sèvres, though essential to the proper furnishing of milady's boudoir and milord's dining-table, were exorbitantly expensive. It was indeed a Frenchman, a silversmith from Liège named Nicholas Sprimont, who, probably after a period of experiment by others unknown, put the factory on a firm footing round the year 1742.

Sprimont's paste is like milky-white glass, shewing tiny points of extra translucency when held against an electric light, covered with a very thick glaze, usually ivory in colour and sometimes bubbled or crazed. Using, sometimes, the mark of an incised triangle, his training as a silversmith led him to imitate silver shapes in the making of jugs, salt-cellars, vases, coffee-pots and so on, many left 'in the white' or, like the famous *goat and bee* cream-jugs, offered white or enamelled. Towards the end of the period a new mark was introduced an anchor, in relief on a tiny round or oval pad of clay. During these early years little that was ambitious was attempted. Enamelling was kept at a minimum, and the typical Chelsea trick of covering defects in the glaze, or firing cracks, with tiny enamelled insects or leaves indicates that firing was a very chancy operation.

The finest period of Chelsea china making, during which the mark was a tiny anchor in red, lasted from about 1750 until about 1760. An improvement in the wares, encouraged by the valuable patronage of George II, was made possible by the invention of a new paste, harder, more easily manageable, colder looking, and shewing patches, not points, of extra translucency which we call *moons*. A distinguishing feature of plates, dishes etc. of the period is the presence beneath the bases of three or four of the spur marks mentioned in a previous chapter. The early years of this fine period saw the perfection of the rarest of all Chelsea wares, the tiny ètuis, scent-bottles and boxes known as *Chelsea Toys*, which were eagerly collected by King George himself. The enamel colours have an indefinable, soft pastel-like appearance, and the characteristic little bouquets and sprays of flowers, and the little insects, are drawn with an almost tremulous but painstaking care. This style was copied from Meissen porcelain, as were most of the decorative styles, the Japans and the Imari designs being copied not direct from the Oriental but from the German 'translations'. This was the period also of wonderfully bold and accurate painting of *botanical* or *Hans Sloane* flowers, and of detailed painting of Aesop's Fable subjects by the celebrated porcelain decorator Jefferyes Hamett O'Neale.

In about 1758 the paste was still further strengthened by the addition of bone-ash, resulting in a body which is chalky in colour, more translucent, and covered with a clear but greenish-tinged glaze which always had a tendency towards serious crazing. This paste was used throughout the ensuing *gold anchor* period (the 1760s) and into the years after the factory was taken over by Derby in 1770. It may be that the red anchor was changed into a gold one in keeping with the greater emphasis on splendid decoration which marks the period. Much of it was inspired by Sèvres, in particular the invention and use of beautiful ground colours, the finest of which are *Rose Pompadour* (claret) and *Mazarine Blue* (the *Bleu-de-Roi* of the French decorators). The latter is seen to particularly lovely effect when it carries intricate decoration in gold and when it is contrasted with white reserves of flowers, birds, Oriental figures, fruit, or figure subjects in the idealised styles of Boucher or Watteau.

Under William Duesbury's management, from 1770 until 1783, the wares of what is known as the Chelsea-Derby period were no longer intended to be the prerogative of Society, but were designed to appeal to a wider less, sophisticated public. Decoration became much more sober, often even severe, though still in the French style, with an emphasis on festoons and sprigs of flowers often allied to classical urns and palish royal blue borders in a somewhat incongruous style. Where as early Chelsea blue and white is exceedingly rare and confined to two or three patterns a great deal was now made, of superlative quality, for Duesbury had always favoured its production at his own Derby factory.

Fine figure making began early at Chelsea, in the shape of exquisitely modelled and splendidly decorated birds, inspired by the engravings in the *History of Uncommon Birds* by George Edwards, and marked with the raised anchor. Red anchor models, more ambitious and yet still finely modelled as permitted by the new paste, were naturally copied from the Meissen ones which it was intended they should replace in public favour, and it is noticeable that the originals are less pleasing in appearance than the copies, on account of the mellowness of the Chelsea paste and glaze. Enamels are delicate and they were used with restraint, with sparing use of gilding. Bases are plainly rectangular, cushion-shaped or circular and flat, in each case bearing applied flowers and leaves in low relief. Among the more ambitious groups, some of them over 14 inches in height, mention may be made of the *Maypole Group* (featuring six rustic figures) and the *Chinese Musicians*.

Figures of the gold anchor period are characterised by the prolific use of brilliant colour, much fine gold, and extravagantly scrolled rococo bases. The modeller made the most of the perfected, easily manageable paste. Thus, groups or figures which are sometimes upwards of 21 inches in height (such as the famous *Roman Charity*) stand upon heavily scrolled bases, the abundant bocage is lush and covered with flowers, and drapery and dresses are enamelled and splendidly gilded with crowded floral diapers and brocades. Only, whereas the red anchor figures express movement and vitality, these later models are comparatively lifeless and stiff.

PLATE 99 Chelsea Scent Bottle.   A
beautiful little piece of the 'Chelsea Toy'
family, since it is but two and a quarter
inches in height; it is from the red–
anchor period, around 1755. The apple is
coloured in puce and white, and the leaf
knop is green.

PLATE 100 A Set of Chelsea Vases. A very lovely set of vases and cove
of the gold-anchor period, *circa* 1760–65. The ground colour is pale turquois
with enamelled flowers in the panels. The four busts modelled upon th
central piece represent the four Seasons.

PLATE 101 Chelsea Round Dish. The work of Jefferyes Hamett O'Neale, the 'Fable Painter', is here found together with delicately painted 'Meissen flowers'. The piece is beautifully and sharply moulded, clearly with the reserved decoration on the border in mind; it dates to the red anchor period, about 1755. The apparently haphazard flower-decoration was in reality carefully planned, with its clever use of large leaves, and the whole design is so restrained as to enhance the nature of the porcelain body.

PLATE 102 Chelsea Tea Wares. Thinly-potted
examples of reticently enamelled tea
ware of the red anchor period,
circa 1755, The colourful bird decorations
are in the "naturalistic" style.

PLATE 103   Chelsea Plate.   A fine clean
example of the extremely rare Chelsea
underglaze-blue decoration of the period
circa 1755–60, which is marked with a large
blue anchor. The design is in the Chinese
style, of such quality and painted in such
a beautiful cobalt blue that it is clear that
the rarity of Chelsea 'blue and white'
is not due to any technical difficulties
that might have been encountered.

PLATE 105 Chelsea Candlestick Figures.
A pair of bocage candlestick figures of
the red-anchor period, about 1755. The
bases are modelled in the scrolled
rococo style, edged with pale sky-blue
and picked out in gold, and the pale yellow
breeches and skirt are reticently sprigged
in purple—in contrast to the usual elaborate brocading common on later figures.

PLATE 104 Chelsea Figure of a Bird. A
very lovely figure of a Guan, made about
1751, and bearing the raised red-anchor
mark which may be clearly seen upon the
base beneath the tail. The illustration shews
the typical base with its little applied
flowers and the good, vigorous modelling,
but it cannot shew the brilliant enamelling
which is a feature of this kind of early ware.

PLATE 106   Chelsea Figures.   Figures of
gold-anchor period tend towards over-
elaboration in form and decoration, but
these models of a Chinaman and Companion are comparatively restrained in spite
of the splendid brocading in enamels and
gold. They date from about 1765.

PLATE 107   An Interesting Comparison. Here we see three versions of the same model, showing how the early porcelain makers used one original, in this case the Meissen figure on the left, and adapted it to their own styles. The centre figure bears the anchor and dagger mark of Bow, and the third belongs to the Chelsea red-anchor period, and bears that mark.

PLATE 108 Chelsea Tureen. Tureens of
all sizes were made at Chelsea, particularly
in the likeness of animals, birds, fishes and
vegetables. This finely modelled and
enamelled carp-tureen bears the red anchor
of the period 1755–60, and it is no less than
nineteen and a quarter inches long.

LUND'S BRISTOL AND
WORCESTER PORCELAIN

There was never a period when excellent porcelain was not made at Worcester, for from the very beginning the management, under Dr. John Wall and William Davis, a chemist, enjoyed the possession of a perfected recipe for making a good, fritt-paste porcelain which contained a high proportion of soapstone or steatite. The result was a very strong yet very manageable body, resistant to boiling water, and greenly translucent. The glaze is glossy, very thin and clear, it never crazed, and is colourless except for a slight tinge of blue on blue and white wares.

The paste and glaze were evolved and perfected before 1750 in Bristol, in a factory situated in the neighbourhood of Redcliffe Backs. The building was formerly a glass house owned by a man named Lowdin (which is the reason why this early porcelain was once known as *Lowdin's Bristol*), but the actual proprietor after its change of use was Benjamin Lund, whose name is now properly given to it. There is some confusion concerning the wares he made, but the raised marks of *Bristoll*, *Bristol* or *Wigorn* on a class of sauce-boats and cream-jugs, moulded with floral festoons with rococo handles, white, painted in underglaze blue, or enamelled in Chinese style, sets them apart as his work. In addition we may include a series of small hexagonal bottles, some vases and covers, a few tea-pots and other tea wares which bear Chinese decoration in the form of birds, flowers and wheatsheaf designs and landscapes, all outlined as it were with a single hair of the brush and filled in with jewel-like enamels including aubergine, blue, yellow, iron-red, turquoise, white, and a very lovely transparent green.

Dr. Wall's company bought up the Lund concern lock, stock and barrel, and moved everything to Worcester between June 1751 and July 1752. It is understandable that it is impossible to distinguish between wares made at Bristol and Worcester during that period but, many of them were of the moulded variety, including tea wares fluted, ribbed, or bearing delicate floral patterns in low relief, large tureens with dolphin handles, and lipless jugs moulded in the form of overlapping cabbage leaves of the kind later supplied with mask lips. During these early years the standard was set for the whole of the *Wall* or *First Period*, for the perfect paste and glaze, the neat, careful and thin potting, and for the decoration which was always impeccable and which ran the gamut of every conceivable style.

Worcester made a speciality of underglaze blue painted and printed wares, at first in the Chinese style with an occasional exact copy of a K'hang Hsi design, but later on in the Meissen taste with flowers and insects, in which case the crossed swords mark was also often copied. Otherwise, blue painted wares, comprising every sort of moulded domestic ware, openwork baskets, and ambitious vases and garnitures, bear the blue open crescent, the script W, the fretted square, or one of a large variety of workmen's symbols. It should be noted, however, that a large proportion of blue and white, painted or printed, is unmarked. Powder-blue wares with reserves of simple Chinese landscape are usually marked with four or six imitation Chinese characters. The Worcester underglaze blue is distinctive, often nearing dark indigo, sometimes paler and very like the true Chinese sapphire, but never with any trace of violet.

An enormous amount of blue printed wares was made, its manufacture following closely upon the introduction of printing in overglaze black, lilac, puce or brown about 1756. Robert Hancock, the engraver responsible, produced many prints, the best known of which include the *King of Prussia*, the *Tea Party*, *Parrot and Fruit*, *Milkmaids* and many versions of the *Panini Ruins*, but for the most part new ones, engraved in less detail, were evolved for the blue printing process. Much ware was sent up the Severn to Caughley to be printed in blue at Turner's factory, so that we often find pieces obviously made of the Worcester paste which bear the violet-toned printing of the Shropshire factory. As regards overglaze printing in black, an interesting class of ware comprises pieces which were over-enamelled in colours, with gilding, in the Giles London studios.

The first coloured wares were based on Chinese designs, ranging from the simply and conventionally floral to good copies of the *famille rose* or arrangements of Chinese figures (*Long Elizas*) in garden or domestic surroundings, at best in reserves upon elaborately brocaded and diapered grounds.

Soon after 1755 the influence of Meissen crept in, and we find an increasing use of the various floral treatments mentioned in a previous chapter. A very strong blue (*dry blue*) was introduced into the extensive Worcester palette at about this time, used for the accurately detailed painting of bouquets and sprays of garden flowers. It is seen in conjunction with other enamels (particularly upon scale-blue wares), but it is at its best when used alone, with or without reticent honey gilding.

The splendour of the First Period reached its peak when, after about 1770, the introduction of Sèvres styles followed the influx of skilled artists from Chelsea. The diversity of styles is such that we have no space here to describe them exhaustively. Quite briefly therefore, the main classes of decoration are as follows: Scaled grounds, notably in blue but rarely in other colours, with reserves of flowers, exotic birds, Watteau figures and Chinese figures, in ascending order of rarity; perfected Japan patterns and Kakiemon designs; glorious coloured grounds of claret, apple or pea-green, turquoise and yellow; and purely French arrangements of hop-trellis, festoons of flowers and leaves, and ribbons. In addition, a great deal of specialised painting was done by artists, nameless for the most part, who worked in the Giles studio and elsewhere.

Dr. John Wall died in 1776, and in 1783 the business was bought by the London agent, Thomas Flight, for his sons Joseph and John. Thus began the *Flight Period*, though in fact there were several different partnerships of the members of the Flight family with Martin Barr, who joined them in 1793.

Lund's Bristol and Worcester Porcelain

The other great early nineteenth-century Worcester factory was that founded by a Flight painter named Robert Chamberlain, who left to form his own company in 1786. Together these two concerns, using a series of perfected pastes which quickly replaced the old steatite body, concentrated for the most part on the splendid painting of flowers, landscapes and figure subjects, with lavish use of the new mercury gilding. They had the patronage of Royalty, and produced many important services, many of them decorated by the trained, specialist painters who were now employed. In 1840 the two factories were amalgamated, and after a short period of Kerr and Binns proprietorship (1852–62) the present Royal Worcester Porcelain Company was formed. A third factory, Graingers, established in 1801, was taken over in 1888.

For some mysterious reason very few figures were made during the First Period, and the models known, which are exceedingly rare, may be very shortly listed. They are a Sportsman and Companion, *La Nourrice*, a Gardener and Companion, and a pair of Turks. This branch of ceramics was ignored also by the Flights, but at Chamberlains a series of figures in the biscuit, glazed white, and enamelled was made, including dogs, sheep and deer, boys in pantaloons and crinolined girls.

PLATE 109 Lund's Bristol Vase and Mug. This small hexagonal vase and cylindrical mug shew the neat potting, the careful drawing and the fine enamelling of the early Lund's Bristol porcelain, dating from about 1750. Both are decorated in *famille-verte* colours, in the Chinese style.

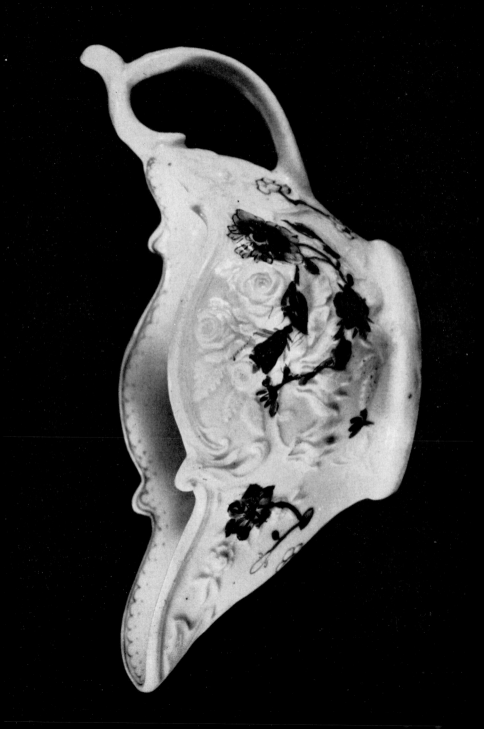

Dating from about 1760–65, this specimen illustrates admirably the haphazard placing of enamelled decoration upon a moulded surface which bears no relation to it. The same moulding, one of many used at Worcester, is often found in underglaze-blue-painted form. The piece is five and three quarter inches long.

PLATE III Worcester Sauce-boats. These three sauce-boats, crisply moulded and painted in underglaze blue, were made *circa* 1760, and offer a reason why there are collectors who specialise in them and in their enamelled counterparts.

PLATE 113 Worcester Dessert Plate. The illustration shews the skilled placing of the design, but it cannot give justice to the brilliant enamelling, which utterly belies its age. In fact, it was applied about 1765 by an anonymous artist who is known as the 'sliced fruit painter', and who worked in James Giles's London studio.

LATE 112 Worcester Vase and Cover. This fifteen-inch-high, xagonal vase represents the height of Worcester attainment in derglaze-blue-painted decoration. The panels on the sides of the dy are in a Chinese style as translated by Meissen, but the simple per borders and landscape vignettes of the neck and cover are pure inese. Vases of this kind may be dated around 1765-70, but the rping which is visible even in the illustration shews that technical ficulties in the potting of such large pieces had by no means been ercome. The mark on the vase and inside the cover is the Meissen ossed swords.

PLATE 114 Worcester Tankard. The bell-shaped tankard or mug,
with its glazed rim and grooved loop-handle, is one of Worcester's
most attractive forms. This example has decoration of root
ornament in puce, reserved on the rare and lovely yellow ground,
and was made about 1765. It is four and five-eighth inches high.

PLATE 115   Worcester Oval Dish.   A typical and fine example of the splendid decoration of the period 1770–75. The border is dark mazarine-blue enriched with gold, and the landscape is attributed to Jefferyes Hamett O'Neale, the 'Fable Painter', an independent outside decorator who also probably worked for some time at the Giles London studio. The fruit and bird painting, in a rich style often found on Worcester porcelain, was probably applied by another hand. The mark is an open blue crescent.

PLATE 116 Worcester Tureen, Cover and
Stand. Decorated in underglaze blue and
enamels in a pattern based on Japanese Imari
ware. This is one of the most elaborate
of the Worcester 'Japans', and is referred to
in the 1769 Catalogue as 'old mosaic japan
pattern'. It can be dated to about 1770.

PLATE 117 Chamberlains Worcester
Figure Few figures were made at Worcester
until the Chamberlain period, and this small
example is marked in red script *Ju*
Breeched, Chamberlains. It dates from about
1810–15, and the same model was made in
white biscuit. The round base is typical
of Worcester figures, and the occasional
crazing of the period is clearly visible

PLATE 119 Worcester Vase and Cov
The potting of these great hexago
vases, sixteen and a half inches in heig
was extremely hazardous, and most
somewhat warped. The decoration is of
splendid exotic bird-and-insect vari
of the 1770s, in this case reserved
a mazarine-blue grou

PLATE 118 Worcester Dish. A fine
Chamberlain's Worcester piece of the
1820–40 period. The juxtaposition of the
enamelled view of the Houses of Parliament
and the typical, applied sea-shells and moss,
vividly enamelled in true colours, may be
considered incongruous, but the whole is a
technical tour-de-force of the highest
standard. The dish is thirteen and a quarter
inches long.

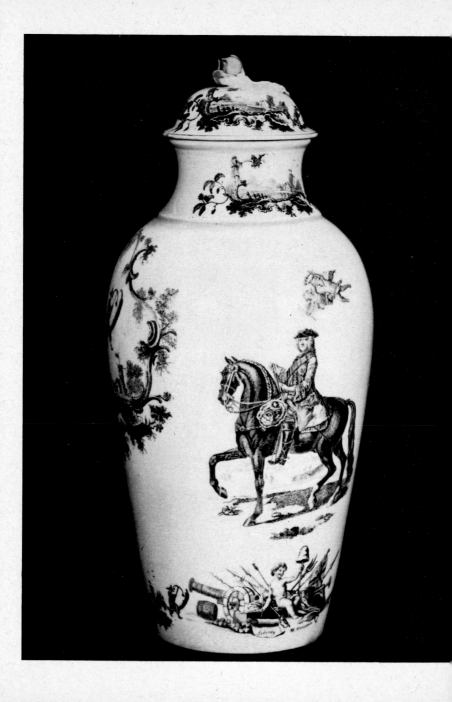

DERBY PORCELAIN

The Derby factory was owned from some time shortly after 1750 by William Duesbury (at first in partnership with John Heath and Andrew Planché), a skilled porcelain painter and acute business man, until his death in 1786. It was then taken over by his son in partnership with Robert Bloor, and was finally closed down in 1848, after a period during which there was a marked decline in the high artistic standards set up and maintained by the founder. With the later Derby factories, one owned by Bloor's clerk, William Locker and, later, by Stevenson and Hancock, and the other, an entirely separate concern founded in 1877 and still in existence, we shall not here concern ourselves; by and large, at least until recent years, the old styles were continued, but their wares are obviously not of great interest to the collector.

Duesbury was undoubtedly a very successful man – he was able to take over the Chelsea, Bow and Longton Hall factories – and his aim was to meet the demand for adequately decorated porcelain of a sensible kind. For that reason, we may suppose, he seldom attempted to copy or to rival the successes of other factories. Nevertheless, it was natural that when the Chelsea artists came to Derby, after the closure of the London factory in 1782, there was a sudden spate of more elaborate and splendid wares, not of services, but of specimen cabinet pieces, painted by specialists such as Billingsley, 'Jockey' Hill, Askew, Withers, the Brewers and Boreman, which could be preserved as works of art behind glass.

Identification of the earliest Derby is difficult, but apparently the paste was glassy and chalky white, thinly and clearly glazed, with a pronounced yellow translucency. Blue painting was done on a large scale (though few patterns can be definitely identified) in a pale tone of blue sometimes inclined to violet, and accompanied occasionally by the mark of a script capital N, incised or painted in blue. As regards underglaze blue printing, although Holdship, in charge of the printing department at Worcester, was at Derby between 1764 and 1769, presumably in order to introduce the process, very few specimens are identifiable, and we can assume only that the paste or glaze, or both were unsuited to transfer printing underglaze. In the sphere of polychrome decoration we do not find the variety that is found upon Worcester wares, and indeed Chinese styles were neglected in favour of those of Meissen. Examples are to be seen, for instance, in the distinctive work of the

ATE 120 Worcester Vase and Cover. This piece is twelve inches h, printed in overglaze black and overpainted in colours. There is equestrian portrait of George II under two cupids bearing laurel and m, a trophy below inscribed *Liberty* with the word 'Worcester' tween the monogram, RH, and an anchor; the other side has a group warships between two identical chinoiserie scenes; on the cover small similar scenes. The printing is attributed to Robert Hancock.

'Moth Painter', whose insects are accompanied by flowers in that style, and who also painted landscapes and birds. Another artist painted thinly stalked flowers in exceedingly pale enamels which seem to have sunk deeply and flatly into the glaze.

Between 1770 and 1784 were the years of what is called the Chelsea-Derby period, when much that was best of Chelsea decoration was adapted at Derby, in particular the Sèvres styles and the use of fine ground colours in turquoise and claret, and of a lapis-lazuli blue (*Derby* or *Smith's blue*) that was paler than the Chelsea mazarine and which replaced it. Many fine Japan patterns were copied from Worcester, and much use was made of festoons and sprays of flowers, urns and classical figures. The lovely *gold stripes* ground appears in this period, the gold lines straight or wavy, and sometimes scattered with flower-sprigs. Little underglaze blue painting was done (and we remember that at Chelsea it was virtually ignored), but what there was is comparable with the best found on Worcester wares.

Ground colours were continued during the following period (1784 to about 1810) when the mark used was the well-known crown and crossed batons, accompanied by magnificent specialised brushwork upon a white, very translucent paste which sometimes crazed. William 'Quaker' Pagg's flowers are outstanding, full-sized and true to nature, Billingsley's wiped-out highlights on his roses are seen on an occasional, special service, and we admire the crimson or grey cupids of Richard Askew, Richard Dodson's colourful bird painting and the almost miniature-like landscapes of Zachariah Boreman and John and Robert Brewer. Under Bloor's management financial troubles necessitated an emphasis on quantity rather than quality, and a cheaper bone-ash paste was introduced. Nevertheless, there was still much good decoration, notably by Moses Webster, a flower-painter whose individual work in the old style contrasts favourably with the conventional, rather flat-looking bouquets of Edwin and Horatio Steele.

Because so many Derby figures were made either in the Chelsea style or, later, in the actual Chelsea moulds, there is often confusion between the products of the two factories, particularly since the late pastes are very similar. Unmistakeably Derby, however, are two distinct classes of figures – those early ones which have a narrow band of unglazed paste beneath the base (the *dry edge* class) and those made between about 1755 and 1770 which have three or four dirty-looking, unglazed patches (*patch marks*) caused by the pads of clay supporting the pieces in the kiln. Chelsea Derby figures, apart from being decorated in enamels which compare favourably with those used in earlier years, commonly bear incised pattern numbers.

Some twenty years after white biscuit figures had been introduced at Sèvres in 1751 (and much collected by Madame Pompadour) Duesbury was able to advertise his own versions of them, made in a smooth, ivory-toned paste,

PLATE 121 Derby Heart-shaped Dish.
The underglaze-blue decoration upon
this dish, of the period *circa* 1760, is in one
of the styles peculiar to the factory. The
key-fret border is distinctive, and the
Chinese water-scene is obviously a haphazard composition of the kind of Oriental
motifs which Europeans had learnt to
recognize and expect—the pagodas, the
exotic trees, the single flower spray,
the fence and the bridge.

Derby Porcelain

and bearing the merest trace of glaze which was due to kiln conditions and which did not in any way hide details of the modelling. The finest work in this regard was done by the modellers John James Spengler and Pierre Stephan, whose figures are outstandingly clear-cut and delicate.

PLATE 122 Chelsea-Derby Round Dish.
The anchor and D-mark in gold denotes a
date between 1770 and 1782, and the decora-
tion is typical of the period; there are the
border of bright 'Derby Blue', the festoons,
the garlanded urn and the carefully painted
insects.

PLATE 123   Chelsea-Derby Sauce-Boat.
Nothing could be finer than the underglaze-
blue-painted decoration upon this handsome
sauce-boat, made about 1770 in a silver shape
peculiar to Chelsea and Derby. The paste
is clear and white, the glaze colourless,
and the blue a brilliant sapphire. The
Chinese brocaded patterns and the flower
sprays are beautifully drawn, and inside
is a Chinese diaper border and a landscape.

PLATE 124 Derby Plate. A very fine
example of the fruit painting of Thomas
Steele, who worked at Derby between 1815
and about 1840. He preferred to work on
flat surfaces such as this, and his work is
usually accompanied by this kind of
arabesque gilded border, the finest of which
were done by a gilder named Thomas Till.

PLATE 125 Derby Cup and Saucer. A Derby chocolate cup
saucer delightfully decorated with four panels, alternating la
scapes with sprays of flowers in multicolour on a brilliant ye
ground. The panels are separated with wide bands of white, ri
gilded with a circle pattern, and this is repeated at the rims w
are undulating. The cup is moulded and has two scrolled white han
outlined with gilding. The pieces were made *circa* 1790 and
marked with a crown over a cross and a D in underglaze puce. The
is three inches high, and the saucer six and one eig

PLATE 126 Derby Plate. Of the period around 1820, this is a good example of Richard Dodson's brightly colourful bird-painting, within a gold arabesque border by Thomas Till. Dodson's birds are semi-naturalistic, a cross between the earlier exotic birds of Worcester and the rather stiff, posed European birds of Meissen.

PLATE 127   Derby Parrots.   Derby birds of any kind are uncommon,
and the painting upon them is usually inferior to that upon similar
Chelsea models. These parrots are enamelled in green and mottled
yellow, with puce and yellow on their wings. They date from about
1755, and are eight and a half inches high.

PLATE 128 Chelsea-Derby Figure. A figure of a Drummer made about 1780. As usual with figures of the period, the pattern book number, in this case, ___ incised in the base. Apparently this specimen is one of a pair, since the factory reference under the number is to 'Pipe and Tabor' figures

PLATE 129 Derby White Biscuit Group. A very fine white-biscuit group, made about 1795, is entitled 'Two Bacchantes adorning Pan', and was modelled by Spengler after a design by Angelica Kauffmann, engraved by F. Bartolozzi. The total height is thirteen inches

PLATE 130 Bloor Derby Jug. A printed
mark in red dates this jug as of the Bloor
period—probably made between 1825 and
1830. Were it not for the presence of the
mark it could equally well be credited to
Coalport or Rockingham, though the pale,
yellow-green ground might be a deciding
factor in Derby's favour.

LOWESTOFT PORCELAIN

It must be made clear at the outset that no true Lowestoft porcelain is of the kind which was given the name of 'Chinese Lowestoft' in the years before serious collecting began. How the myth was born does not really matter, and it suffices to say that 'Chinese Lowestoft' wares are in reality quite ordinary Chinese export wares of indifferent quality, whereas true Lowestoft porcelain was made of a fritt paste containing bone-ash having an almost colourless translucency, covered by a slightly blued glaze.

I make no apology for using again, as I have used many times elsewhere, the expression 'toy-like' as an apt description of Lowestoft wares. Everything seems to have been on a small scale, the humble beginnings in 1757 when a chemist named Robert Browne set up his factory, apparently without any considerable financial backing, the absence of advertising or public sales, and even the comparatively small size of many articles of domestic ware, tea-bowls and saucers in particular. Apparently the factory employed no specialist painters, we find no splendid decoration and almost no gilding, and the blue painting was done by girls. Nevertheless, Lowestoft porcelain is distinctively homely and British in some indefinable way, even when the design upon it is in the Chinese style.

As at Worcester, many early wares were moulded, sometimes copied from the models used at that great factory, but occasionally in quite original styles, such as a design of three radial bands of trellis pattern and circular medallions, and an all-over floral pattern in low relief which is found on mask-lip jugs, partly covered by landscape in the Chinese style painted in underglaze blue of almost indigo tint, the rather granulated appearance of which is best observed in the only Lowestoft scale-blue pattern, in the shape of spirally radiating panels. On the other hand, considerable use was made of powder-blue, in the manner of Worcester, Bow and Caughley, with round and fan-shaped reserves of simple Chinese landscape or, very rarely, irregularly shaped ones. Other favourite patterns include the Berlin (and Copenhagen) *Immortelle* arrangement of flower-sprays, plain or ribbed, the Worcester *peony* design with its accompanying *pineapple* border, various arrangements of *rock* motif and flowering shrubs, and simple Chinese landscapes. Peculiar to Lowestoft was the practice of painting dates, names, and the inscription 'A Trifle from Lowestoft' not only in blue but also in colours on such pieces as mugs, tea-pots, jugs and inkwells.

Blue printing was done at Lowestoft, but a characteristic hesitancy of line shews that the factory had no engraver of the calibre of Worcester's Hancock. Indeed, the difficulty of depicting mass by means of close shading and hatching had often to be overcome by adding extra blue pigment to the printed design. Comparatively little coloured decoration was attempted, the commonest pattern being root-ornament design (the *Redgrave* pattern) in opaque blue, bright emerald green and red. Other patterns include bouquets of flowers, crudely drawn and featuring two globular roses placed back to back, Chinese mandarin patterns sometimes reserved in a diapered ground, an occasional simple armorial design, and various arrangements of scrolls and/or flower-sprigs. Much Lowestoft ware is wrongly credited to the New Hall factory, and vice-versa, but a study and comparison of the two pastes, the soft and the hard, should enable the collector to distinguish between the two porcelains.

In common with other porcelains, Lowestoft specimens have certain characteristics which help in their identification. The undersides of the bases of domestic wares commonly sag down almost to a point, rims and flanges of tea and coffee-pots are glazed inside (unlike their unglazed Worcester and Caughley counterparts), and tea-pots are almost invariably rectangular in the Chinese style. Also copied from the Chinese are short blue or enamelled brush-strokes on either side of handle terminals. For marks Lowestoft used the Worcester crescent and crossed swords in tiny form, and a series of numbers between 1 and 30 was apparently allocated to the blue-painters.

No figures have as yet been positively credited to the factory, if we perhaps except a series of small sheep, lambs, cats and swans which do not readily fall into any Staffordshire category.

PLATE 131   Lowestoft Tankard.   A typically toy-like tankard, only three and a half inches high, painted in underglaze blue in the Chinese style, and dating from about 1765. Notice the blue strokes on either side of the handle terminals, a characteristic of Lowestoft vases, copied from the Chinese. It is marked with the painter's numeral, 5.

PLATE 132   Lowestoft Bowl.
The clear-cut moulded design of
this bowl, made about 1765, is
peculiar to the factory. The underglaze-blue landscapes are neatly
drawn and exactly fitted to the
shapes of the reserves (even to the
little patches of water-weed that
fit the bulges), and the borders are
of a type common on Lowestoft
'blue and white'.

PLATE 133 Lowestoft Tea Wares.
The enamelled decoration on
these pieces, dating from 1760,
contrasts significantly with that
which characterises the so-called
'Chinese Lowestoft'. The painting
on the pieces on the upper shelf
is nevertheless in the Chinese style,
while those below have a clear
kinship with Meissen. Notice that
Lowestoft and Worcester shared
the same globular shape of teapot.

PLATE 134 Lowestoft Porcelain. Decorated in the Chinese style in underglaze blue and of the period *circa* 1757–60. The placing of the handle on the coffee-pot is unusual, but the borders of Chinese diaper and flowers are very typical of Lowestoft.

PLATE 135 Lowestoft Jug and Teapot. The date of these pieces, about 1765, makes them contemporary with Worcester ones of similar form, but the decoration is very different. The net diaper around the neck of the jug, the kick-out of the handle at the lower terminal, the conical knob to the teapot lid, and the bouquet of flowers (very much in the Caughley style) are the distinguishing features, apart from the colourless translucency of both pieces.

PLATE 136   Lowestoft Coffee-Pot.   A very graceful and sensible
coffee-pot made about 1770–75, decorated with Chinese landscapes in
underglaze blue on a powder-blue ground. It is interesting to note
that the author purchased this actual piece some twenty years ago for £7
at an auction, since when it has passed through many hands to be
finally sold for nearly £200.

LONGTON HALL PORCELAIN

So far as we know it is a strange fact that the only early porcelain-making factory in the Potteries was founded about 1750 by William Littler, the salt-glazed earthenware maker, who was helped by William Jenkinson, the apparent possessor of a workable formula. Despite the advantages that one might suppose its position would have given to it, the factory was short-lived, and was closed down in 1760.

Jenkinson's paste was a glassy one, very like that of early Chelsea. Its translucency is not of a constant colour, varying between green and yellow, often showing moons, and the glaze is thick, and apt to collect in bluish blobs like candle-fat around and under bases, which on that account often had to be ground level. Potting is markedly clumsy, pieces are often remarkably heavy for their size, and hardly a piece but is warped or fire-cracked.

Many of the early wares were moulded in the shapes of overlapping leaves, and consist mainly of dishes, crude baskets, pickletrays, tureens and stands, and other accessories rather than services. For the most part decoration was carried out in washes of *Littler's Blue*, the almost opaque ground colour which is so characteristic of Longton Hall wares, used either in panels by itself or in combination with elementary but carefully drawn flower-sprays in blue or in enamels. It was clearly very difficult to prevent this distinctive blue from running with the glaze. Many pieces which are decorated with it, and with nothing else, seem rather uninteresting, but we are reminded by an occasional trace of gold that it was often originally enhanced by patterning in unfired size gilding.

Jenkinson left the concern in 1753, whereupon there was an improvement both in the quality of the wares and in the decoration upon them. Intricate moulding and occasional openwork on rims was attempted. A much more extensive palette included pink, orange, red, blue and yellow-greens, and opaque blue. Some good exotic-bird painting was done in pleasantly subdued enamels, seen at best, with butterflies painted upon the rims, on some very proficient plates with moulded strawberry borders, the so-called *strawberry plates*. Among the occasional, exceptionally ambitious pieces three in the Victoria and Albert Museum in London are noteworthy, a moulded jug with a ground of Littler's Blue upon which are reserved panels containing a Watteau idyllic scene and flowers, and a pair of elaborate vases with ropetwist handles, on high-footed scrolled bases, painted in enamels with Chinese scenes after Pillement.

The last three years of the factory's life were clearly most difficult, and the emphasis was on easily produced wares for the most part painted in underglaze blue, mainly tea and coffee sets, and heavy cylindrical tankards with moulded reserves on either side, and the characteristic Longton Hall double-scrolled handles. No printing was attempted, and indeed the decorative policy of the factory was seemingly quite unlike that of any other, following as it did no plausible scheme of progress through the tastes of the Chinese, Meissen, and Sèvres, but choosing styles haphazardly.

Figures were made at Longton Hall, though the *short* paste, difficult to manipulate, was at first quite unsuitable. The earliest belong to a now identified class known by the name of *snow man*, comprising over thirty models, in the contemporary style of Chelsea, hollow, with unglazed bases pierced by small conical holes. The usual blobs of glaze are often present. With the improvement in paste about 1753 the modelling greatly improved – to such an extent that many figures have in the past been credited to Chelsea, having the same Meissen origin. In fact, they are betrayed by their colouring, which includes a strong pink that was often used to pick out the lines of scrolled rococo bases. Strangely enough, and perhaps in a last effort to save a sinking ship, the finest work in this regard was done just before the closure. Thus, we may contrast the vigorous, reticently enamelled group *The Dancers* (sometimes called *The Lovers*) mounted high on a rococo base picked out in purple and nearly eleven inches high (Fitzwilliam Museum, Cambridge) with the equally striking set *Continents*, once believed to have been made at Plymouth such is their quality, which are at Temple Newsam, Leeds. These four pieces are over a foot in height, the modelling is outstandingly good, and the decoration most elaborate, with intricately brocaded drapery. Such achievement underlines the tragedy of William Littler, who died in poverty in 1784.

PLATE 137   Longton Hall Plate.   The moulded
border decoration, picked out characteristically in
puce and green, has given the name of 'Strawberry
Plate' to this design. It was made during the middle
period of the factory, between 1754 and 1757.

PLATE 138 Longton Hall Sauce-Boats.
Moulded leaf forms of this kind were made
in large quantities during the middle period,
circa 1754-57, in blue and white and in
colour. In these examples the pale green
leaves have puce veins. They are unusually
large, being no less than nine and a quarter
inches in length.

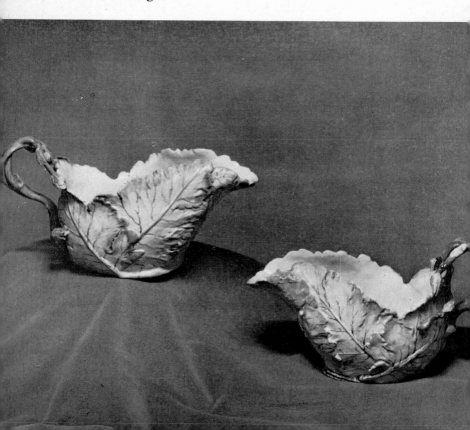

PLATE 139 Longton Hall Teapot. The
rather hesitant style of Longton Hall
flower-painting, with a predominance
of puce enamel, is seen to advantage in
this illustration. The bird's-head spout
is a Longton characteristic, and the piece
may be dated *circa* 1755.

PLATE 140 Longton Hall Leaf Dish.
Here again are the puce-veined, green-
bordered leaves characteristic of Longton
Hall moulded wares. The hesitant brushwork
is of, in this case, an artist known as the
'trembly rose' painter, and can be dated
circa 1755–60.

PLATE 141 Longton Hall Dishes. The peony dish on the right has a yellow centre with pink borders; the green leaves are yellow-bordered, and the twig handle is turquoise. The dish on the left has typical puce veins. Both may be dated *circa* 1755.

PLATE 142 Longton Hall Figures. A rare pair of charming figures
from the Italian Comedy representing Harlequin and Columbine in
dancing poses. Harlequin wears a chequered costume in brilliant reds,
blue, green, yellow and brown, and his wide-brimmed hat is black
with a green feather. In his hand he holds a yellow slapstick.
Columbine wears a décolleté bodice, the sides with a diamond
pattern in red, blue, green and yellow; one sleeve has a similar
pattern and the other is yellow with scattered playing cards. Her hat is
green and her skirt pink with blue spots. Both figures are on mound
bases with applied leaves and flowers, and date from about 1755.

LIVERPOOL PORCELAIN

There is still little that is certainly known about porcelain making in Liverpool, in spite of a great deal of painstaking research and the existence of an enormous quantity of ware which could hardly have been made anywhere else. We do know, however, that between 1755 and 1770 at least a dozen potteries who probably had made delft began to make porcelain, and that certain characteristics of potting and decoration have been accepted as proof of a Liverpool origin. These we will consider, bearing in mind that more and more wares, often of surprisingly fine quality, are constantly being claimed as having been made at one or another of the factories, and that for the pros and cons it is necessary to consult up-to-date specialised literature.

It is certain that a Worcester potter named Robert Podmore joined Richard Chaffers and Philip Christian in 1755, in order to make porcelain from the formula, containing steatite, which he brought with him. Thus, until Chaffers died in 1765, a ware was made that may often be mistaken for Worcester, having the same green translucency, the same glaze, the same neat potting and shapes, and the same kind of pseudo-Chinese decoration in underglaze blue. We look therefore, when in doubt, for an outstanding difference, which is a technical one – whereas a Worcester foot-rim is bluntly triangular in section, that of a Liverpool piece is undercut. After Chaffers died the work continued, but the steatite content of the paste was replaced by bone-ash, resulting in a yellowish translucency, while at the same time the glaze was so blued that it has often collected in a dirty blue 'thundercloud' effect within the foot-rim angle. To this period belong the familiar helmet-shaped cream-jugs with handles whose upper terminals bite the rim in silver style (the *biting-snake* handle) and tea-pots moulded with palm-trees rising from acanthus leaves at the base.

From this beginning porcelain making in Liverpool was developed, until by the end of the century the competition of Wedgwood and Worcester, in particular, brought it virtually to a close. Blue painting was done at every factory, among which were those owned by James and John Pennington, Seth Pennington, William Ball, Reid & Co., Zachariah Barnes and Samuel Gilbody. Most of the ware was in the Chinese style and much was copied from Worcester, with the result that there is an ever-increasing tendency to reclassify a great deal of ware that was once thought to be of undoubted Worcester origin, but which admittedly is not quite up to the usual high standards of that factory. Original designs peculiar to Liverpool include one featuring what appear to be five upright boards with a peony above, a series of conventional floral patterns, with daisy-like flowers having solid blue, round centres and blobbed leaves, a rather lovely arrangement of a peony spray upon which is perched a carefully drawn, long-tailed bird, and a Chinese landscape featuring two little Chinamen so drawn as to resemble toadstools. The *jumping boy* pattern of Bow is often seen. Many Liverpool blue and white wares have an elementary trellis border.

Since Sadler and Green had their printing works in the city it was inevitable that we find overglaze enamel printing on Liverpool porcelain, in black, brown, sepia, red and puce, common patterns including several very like those used at Worcester, such as various versions of *Ruins*, *Tea Party*, *King of Prussia*, *Parrot and Fruit* and *Red Cow* (which as at Worcester was often washed in with colour). As at Worcester, too, underglaze-blue printing followed between 1765 and 1769, on a very large scale, but much inferior in comparison, featuring a very dark blue, wet-looking, that is usually much blurred, and common use of most elaborate scrolled and diapered borders similar to those used at Caughley.

Although one or other of the Liverpool factories was occasionally able to produce polychrome wares equal in appearance to some of the simpler Worcester designs, in particular of the mandarin type, coloured decoration is usually extremely simple, with very little use of gilding or ground colours, with the exception of a streaky, greyish-blue sketchily 'marbled' in gold. Some blue and white wares were embellished with red enamel, and simple Chinese patterns of *Long Elizas* are usually distinguishable from the Worcester cousins by the poor, rather muddy quality of the enamels, and by patches of iron-red shading in the foreground. An unmistakeable Liverpool design of this kind features a Chinaman beckoning to a lady who holds an umbrella.

PLATE 143 Liverpool Bowl. A bowl of the period 1775–80, made by Seth Pennington. The style of decoration, with its blobs of dark blue and typically Liverpool trellis border is characteristic.

PLATE 144 Liverpool Cup and Saucer.
An octagonal cup and saucer made by
Chaffers of a steatite paste similar to that
used at Worcester. The potting is thin and
neat, the paste clear and white, and the
underglaze-blue painting of the finest
quality. The pattern is the well-known
'Jumping Boy' which was used also at Bow.
The date is *circa* 1758–60.

PLATE 145   Liverpool Teapot.   This is
the model of a teapot which was once mistakenly attributed to Longton Hall, partly
because of the moulded strawberry leaves at
the base. It may be dated *circa* 1770–75.

HYENA

PLATE 147 Liverpool Bowl. The exterior of the bowl, seen opposite. The ship mentioned, 'Hyena' was built in 1778.

LATE 146 Liverpool Bowl. inted in colours with the frigate Hyena' and a naval trophy. The terior has the 'Hyena' and other ips on the Mersey seen from idston Hill with the observatory d a windmill in the distance. he diameter is nine and a half ches. Pieces of this kind are usually tributed to Pennington's poetry, d may be dated *circa* 1775–80.

PLATE 148   Liverpool Tea-Bowl and
Saucer.   A number of very similar patterns
of this kind were produced between about
1790 and 1800, featuring the same kind of
shaded tree, the rather dirty enamels, and
the typical border of india-red. The pattern
was probably pure invention on the part of
the decorator, who must have thoroughly
enjoyed painting the little dogs.

SALOPIAN PORCELAIN

Salopian porcelain comprises that which was made at Caughley (pronounced Calfley) from 1772 by Thomas Turner, and at nearby Coalport from 1814 until the closure of the works quite recently.

Speaking by and large the wares made at Caughley bear a striking resemblance to the simpler kinds of Worcester, having a similar steatitic composition (though usually unblued by cobalt and so showing a straw-coloured translucency), a similar though not so brilliant glaze, and an almost equal neatness of potting. In the last regard it is noticeable that whereas a Worcester foot-rim has a wedge-shaped or bluntly triangular section, that of a Caughley piece is usually rectangular, and fairly high.

By far the greater part of the Caughley output was decorated by underglaze blue printing, and we have already mentioned that in fact much Worcester domestic ware was sent up the river by *Severn Trow* (a kind of barge) to be decorated in that manner; thus we may often find a Worcester piece (on the evidence of paste) bearing printed decoration in the style and in the violet-toned blue of Caughley. Peculiar to the factory is a mechanical style of engraving in which water, for example, is rendered in a series of exactly parallel, close-spaced lines. Thomas Turner was himself an engraver, and among his pupils was Thomas Minton, the founder of the great Staffordshire firm, whose work is to be seen in the shape of the Caughley *Broseley Dragon* and *Willow Pattern* printed designs. Other characteristic patterns are the *Fisherman* (or *Cormorant*), the *Cornflower* and the *Pheasant*. The first of these, so far as I know, is never found on Worcester porcelain, though it was occasionally used at Lowestoft. A peculiarity of one Caughley pattern, featuring a large vase of flowers standing before a fence, is that part of the design is washed in by brush with pale underglaze blue. Two border styles are peculiar to the factory and are not, again, found on Worcester porcelain – various versions of intricate diaper, scroll, floral and butterfly arrangements, and a similar kind of pattern interrupted by reserves containing English landscapes or rustic scenes with cattle or sheep. More elaborate copies of Worcester wares include cabbage-leaf, mask-lip jugs (some of them carrying printed views of the iron bridge over the Severn at Ironbridge), butter dishes with covers and stands, and open-sided baskets. The usual Caughley marks on printed ware are the capital C, the word *SALOPIAN* impressed, a series of numerals so disguised as to resemble Chinese characters, and the Worcester crescent.

Little blue painting was done, apart from *Cornflower* and other simple flower spray designs, with an occasional *Long Eliza* composition, but particularly pleasing is a powder-blue pattern featuring alternating radial panels of blue and Chinese emblems. Ordinary Caughley powder-blue plates are of exactly the same design as those made elsewhere. Polychrome decoration is uncommon, and is usually seen in the form of closely-packed bouquets of flowers with pink roses line-shaded in darker red, and leaves sometimes outlined in gold.

In 1799 a former Caughley apprentice named John Rose bought the factory, and by 1814 he had moved everything across the river to Coalport. From the beginning, apparently, he was able to make a very fine, hardish, whitely translucent paste, which was improved still further after Billingsley joined him in 1820. Thus, after that date and for the next thirty years or so porcelain was made which has often been mistaken for that which Billingsley had made at Swansea and Nantgarw.

Among the best pieces of this early Coalport are those which are often given the misleading name of Coalbrookdale (a nearby village famous for ironwork, but not connected in any way with porcelain making), decorated with well-modelled applied flowers painted in a distinctive palette, and with enamelled flower bouquets or landscapes in a style similar to that used at Rockingham and Derby. Otherwise Sèvres styles were favoured, with good bird and flower painting, festoons and swags, urns, and coloured grounds in great variety. We find also some rather gaudy Japans, and a class of domestic ware moulded in low relief and painted with garden flowers.

From about 1850 onwards Rose concentrated upon the use of improved coloured grounds (notably *Bleu-de-Roi*, *Rose Pompadour*, turquoise and several fine greens) together with reserves of the finest painting, lavishly gilded. To this period belong also the well-known mugs bearing flower-painting or landscapes, with inscriptions and dates in gold, and the rather hackneyed *Indian Tree* pattern beloved by all Salopians.

A third factory was set up at Madeley, near Ironbridge, about 1825 by Thomas Martin Randall, a London outside decorator. His porcelain bore an even closer resemblance to that of Sèvres than that made at Coalport, and since he decorated in the French style he was under continuous pressure from the London china dealers to add the Sèvres mark. This he never seems to have done, though he had no objection to decorating French wares, already marked, which were supplied to him *in the white*. In the absence of any mark at all, Madeley porcelain is well-nigh impossible to identify unless the brushwork of his artists is recognised – his nephew John painted colourful birds and so did he himself, Robert Bix Grey specialised in flowers, fruit and birds, and Phillip Ballard's renderings of Watteau subjects are outstandingly delicate. In some of the cottages in Madeley and the neighbouring villages much Madeley porcelain is still hidden away, among it certain lions on cushion bases, one or two of which are marked *T.M.R. MADELEY*. The modelling of these is so good that one wonders whether the handful of unmarked figures usually credited to Coalport, in pious or idyllic shepherd and shepherdess styles, might not have been made at this smaller factory.

PLATE 149 Caughley Tea-wares. Here are three underglaze-blue-printed designs of the period around 1775. The piece on the left features a Chinese garden scene, in the centre is the 'Pheasant' pattern, and on the right is the 'Fisherman' or 'Cormorant' pattern. The last, with its typical Caughley 'cell' border, is found only on Salopian wares, but the other two are found also on Worcester porcelain sent up the river to be printed.

PLATE 150 Caughley Teapot. A polychrome teapot and cover made about
1775–80. The form is exactly that of a
contemporary Worcester teapot, but
distinguishing features are the paste with
its straw-coloured translucency, the less
brilliant glaze, and the style of flower
painting, with the characteristically shaded
petals.

PLATE 151 Coalport Teapot and Cover. This quite unpractical 'Coalbrookdale' specimen bears the mark *SWANSEA* in red, and represents the kind of ware whose value has been much enhanced in the past by misidentification. The quality of the paste and glaze, however, prove a Coalport origin, and it is evident that the pot was made about 1830.

PLATE 153 The Broseley Dragon. One of the earliest Caughley blue-printed patterns, known also as the 'Brosely Blue Dragon' or 'Brosely blue Canton'. It was copied from the Chinese, and a similar design in painted form is to be found on Bow and Worcester vases.

E 152 Coalport Vase and Cover. Coalport porcelain of this
f the period around 1840–60, is often given the name of 'Coal-
ale'. The style is that of Meissen, and the mark, in keeping, is
ssed swords in blue. Because it is made of soft paste it cannot be
en for a continental piece, but its similarity to vases made at
igham might be puzzling. The collector can only study and
he styles and the colouring of the particular applied flowers which
lways used on Coalport wares.

PLATE 154 Madeley Vase. A very fine
example of the exotic-bird painting of
Thomas Martin Randall on his own porcelain, dating from about 1830. The piece
is in Sèvres style, with a dark mazarine-blue
ground patterned in gold. Such specimens,
being unmarked, are often mistaken for
true, soft-paste *Vieux Sèvres* porcelain.

WELSH PORCELAINS

William Billingsley was a perfectionist who never gave up. At a time when others were content to use the bone-ash body which was accepted throughout the industry he persisted in making his own incomparable soft-paste ware whenever he could find financial backing, or wherever someone would employ him.

In the course of his wanderings he went to Worcester, as we have already seen in a previous chapter, and he left there, somewhat under a cloud, to set up a factory in Nantgarw, near Cardiff. At the end of a year, when funds had run out, he was persuaded to go to Swansea, with Samuel Walker his son-in-law, to make his ware in Dillwyn's *Cambrian Pottery*, and for a time all was well. Then, at the end of 1816, when the Worcester company complained of broken contracts, he was forced to leave and to return to Nantgarw. Finally, he left Wales for good in 1820 to go to Coalport, taking his ideas and much of his equipment with him.

Billingsley first used his paste at Pinxton, though he improved upon it as the years passed by. Admittedly it contained bone-ash, but his own special blend of china-clay and a glassy fritt produced a paste as good as that of Sèvres, pure, wonderfully translucent, with no blemish of any kind, covered by a perfect, colourless glaze. Unfortunately, however, it could be produced only at the expense of such kiln losses that it was never a practical proposition.

At Nantgarw, then, Billingsley made wonderful tea and dessert services, decorative tazzas, spill-vases, candlesticks, pen-trays and so on, and a great number of splendidly decorated dishes and plates, many with moulded rims, the patterns of which can be seen and felt clearly on the undersides. Some of this ware he decorated himself, setting the style of the *Billingsley Rose* (and other flowers) in which highlights were wiped out from full colour, not down to the porcelain beneath, but just enough to give the desired effect. He employed decorators too, but much of his porcelain went to be finished in London, to be painted in the readily saleable Sèvres styles. This outside decoration on Nantgarw is not so desirable in the eyes of the collector as that applied in the factory, and it can be recognised by the presence of iridescence which encircles the painting like a halo. In any case, a desirable piece should preferably be marked with the impressed *NANTGARW C.W.* mark, often almost entirely obliterated by the glaze), because otherwise its possessor may never feel absolutely certain that he has not bought an unusually fine piece of Coalport.

Since Dillwyn of Swansea was a business man and less of an idealist than Billingsley, he insisted on changes in the paste, in attempts to reduce kiln losses. About 1816 came the *duck-egg* body, so-called because of its greenish translucency, to be shortly followed by the much cheaper *trident* paste, marked with one or two impressed tridents. This did not please the London dealers, because its yellowish translucency and rather roughly surfaced glaze could not be compared with the Sèvres characteristics for which they looked. Their disapproval naturally meant that they would have none of the new Swansea wares.

Since Billingsley's Nantgarw porcelain was so readily saleable it was natural that at Swansea the same styles were continued. He was probably responsible for the training of painters rather than for technical matters, and known Swansea decorators of exceptional skill included David Evans and William Pollard (fruit and flowers), George Beddow (landscapes), Thomas Baxter (landscapes and garden scenes), and Henry Morris (floral bouquets). Indeed, flower painting is the real glory of Swansea porcelain, and the sight of a properly lighted cabinet of the finest pieces so decorated is an amazingly beautiful and unforgettable experience.

PLATE 155 Nantgarw Plates. The plate on the
left clearly shows the typical Nantgarw moulding,
associated in this case with Thomas Pardoe's
flower-painting. The plate on the right is from
one of the several fine services known either as
'Duke of Gloucester' or 'Duke of Cambridge'.
The pattern is a truly splendid one, featuring panels
of garden flowers reserved on a turquoise or
apple-green ground with *oeil de perdrix* ('pheasant
eye') in gold. These services were decorated in
London probably by Robins and Randell, and
supplied to the Royal household by John Mortlock.
The plate on the left is nine and three quarter inches
in diameter; the one on the right, nine and a quarter.

PLATE 157 Swansea Ice-p
This graceful ice-pail was pain
about 1817–18 by the sa
Thomas Baxter who work
at Worcester and elsewh
The panelled views are rat
large, but their well-desig
shapes and the reticence of
gilding are such that t
detract neither from the sim
lines nor from the pure, glisten
whiteness of the pa

PLATE 156   Nantgarw Plate.
Here is another fine example of
'outside' decoration, in this case
featuring views of Esher Place in
Surrey. The moulding of the
border is not clearly shewn in the
illustration, but its scrolling is
picked out in gold.

P

E.C.

PLATE 158 Swansea Plate. A
lovely combination of a well-
painted harbour scene and a finely
gilded, moulded border painted
with flowers on a 'dotted-gold'
ground. This was made about 1815.

PLATE 159 Swansea Plate. This illustration shews very clearly the Swansea moulding, of the kind seen also on Coalport plates made after Billingsley joined the factory. The lovely flowers were painted by Henry Morris, about 1820. Notice the perfect spacing of the sprigs on the border, apparently haphazard, but executed, in fact, with clever intent.

PLATE 160 Pair of Swansea Vases.
The distinctive shape of these
vases, the quality of the paste and
glaze, and the lovely, naturalistic
flower-painting identify them as
Swansea pieces of the period around
1815–20, although they are unmarked.

ENGLISH TRUE PORCELAINS

While most were content to make some kind of fritt, or 'soft paste' wares, there were those who knew that in some respects such imitations fell far short of the true porcelains made by the Chinese and by the great German factory of Meissen. One such man was William Cookworthy, a Plymouth chemist, who, reputedly by accident, discovered just as Böttger had done, that the body of true porcelain was simply a mixture of china-clay and china-stone. He put his discovery to use in 1768, moved from Plymouth to Bristol in 1770, and in 1773 left the business for his partner, Richard Champion, to carry on. In turn Champion sold out in 1781 to a new company in the Potteries, at New Hall.

Every collector must learn how to distinguish between the hard paste, or true porcelains made at the three centres, and the artificial ones made elsewhere, but it is well-nigh impossible for the differences to be expressed in words. The only way is to handle pieces of both kinds until at length the ability to recognise each will become instinctive. Nevertheless, here are the characteristics to look for. A hard paste does not warm so quickly to the touch, an unglazed portion (such as the exposed edge of a foot-rim) will resist a file or a sharp point, the edge of a fracture will have a glassy appearance with no granulation. The glaze on a piece of hard paste is usually hard, but that upon soft paste is so soft that it may be considerably scratched or even worn away, sometimes together with any enamelled decoration that was upon it. A hard paste glaze, being fired with the paste, has become one with it, but on a soft paste piece it has remained separate and its thickness may sometimes be seen. Enamelled decoration sinks into the glaze on soft paste, but stands proud on true porcelain. The glaze on true porcelain is often disfigured by tiny pits which may be blackened. It is the trained observance of these differences which enables the expert to make an immediate decision, often by touch alone.

To return then, the early Plymouth (and Bristol) true porcelain is like white glass, with a thin, colourless glaze, and the translucency is palely grey. There was a tendency towards warping and fire-cracking – enamels have sometimes flaked off in the course of time, and there is often a perceptible ridging or *wreathing* inside jugs, bowls and so on, left by the potter's fingers. Much early ware was decorated in an almost black underglaze blue with patterns pirated from the soft paste wares, but polychrome decoration is usually of a high standard, in pure, bright enamels, and always reticent and well-balanced. Good flower painting, though simple, with crescent-shaped sprays and an insect or two, Oriental designs of the *Long Eliza* and *famille-verte* types, and naturalistic and exotic birds comprise most of the more usual styles. Cookworthy concentrated on domestic wares in the usual shapes of the period, but with an occasional hexagonal vase, a mantelpiece garniture of beakers and vases, or a salt, or centrepiece, fashioned in the form of tiered scallop-shells.

229

Under Champion a new decorative style was evolved, featuring in particular the typical festoons of flowers, in green alone or in polychrome, the ribbons, and the many arrangements of little sprigs. Many artists, migrant or in the outside studios, painted the same varieties of exotic birds at Plymouth as they did at Worcester – to even better decorative advantage on the intensely white surface. Ground colours were used in combination with very fine gilding.

The removal of the business to New Hall brought with it an apparently instantaneous change in every regard. Concentration was entirely upon utilitarian domestic ware, a new range of tea-pots and cream-jugs was evolved, all of them in characteristic silver shapes of the simpler kind, and ground colours and (with a few outstanding exceptions) gilding was discarded. Patterns are for the most part simple arrangements of sprigs, elementary bouquets, baskets of flowers, and shells, with simple borders of wavy, straight and dotted lines. A common feature is the presence of a strong puce enamel on tea-pot knobs and in the form of dashes, dots or scrolls on handle curves. This kind of almost crude ornamentation was applied to a dirty, grey paste, with a yellow translucency. It is very understandable that in 1810 the making of this kind of porcelain ceased, similar patterns being used on an ordinary bone-ash paste for another fifteen years.

Figures were made from the beginning at Plymouth and Bristol, well-modelled enough, on scrolled or rectangular bases, and in the Chelsea style, though decorated less gaily and fancifully. As on the other wares, however, warping and fire-cracking were common defects. Champion managed to overcome these faults to a certain extent, but decoration on later figures is still never elaborate, while bocage was never used and rococo scrolled bases were discarded. There was naturally no interest in figure making at the New Hall factory.

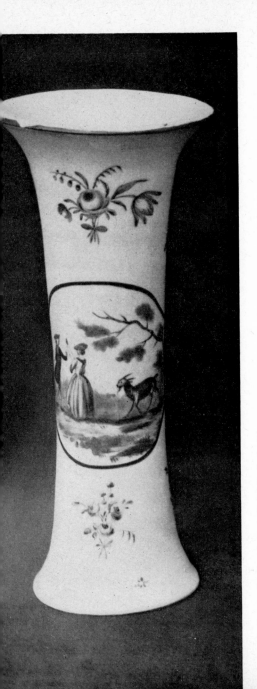

PLATE 161 Plymouth Beaker.
A Plymouth beaker of the period
circa 1765–70. This is perhaps not
an important piece in any way,
but there is something most
appealing about its decoration,
which is reticent and which in no
way detracts from the intrinsic
beauty of the shape. The panel is
in the Watteau style, but with a
humourous twist which is rare in
ceramic decoration.

PLATE 162 New Hall Teapot.
This boat-shaped form is particularly pleasing and practical.
The pattern, in Japan style, is one of
the more elaborate New Hall
ones that are rarely to be found;
it is carried out in red, blue and
gold. The piece was made about
1780.

PLATE 163 Bristol Jug. A stately jug, over
eight inches tall, which was made about 1770 under
Champion's managership, and which was formerly
in the famous Trapnell Collection, according to the
label that, of course, has never been removed.
The rather muddy enamels, particularly the
almost brown tone of the roses, the festoons about
the neck, and a very pronounced 'wreathing' of the
paste inside, are characteristic.

ATE 164   Bristol Plate.   This illustration of a
e of the period *circa* 1770–80 clearly shews typical
ver-painting in the Meissen style, and the
al festoons and ribbon border which are very
racteristic of Bristol wares.

PLATE 165   New Hall Cream-
jugs.   Three typical jugs of the
'hard paste' period of New Hall,
made about 1790. The unmistak-
able features are the moulded
shapes, the elementary style of
flower painting, the rudimentary scale pattern in pink, the
wavy dotted lines, and the puce
decoration upon the handles.

PLATE 166 Bristol Tea Wares. Here are typical tea-wares of the simpler kind, made between 1770 and 1780. Notice the characteristic ogee shape of the handleless tea-bowl. The 'sparrow-beak' jug, so similar in shape to those made at Worcester, might well be considered as a connecting link between well-decorated Bristol and the rough-and-ready wares made at New Hall.

19th CENTURY DEVELOPMENTS

In the previous chapters we have touched upon several early nineteenth-century earthenwares and porcelains, and it has been noted that by and large foreign influence in decoration had by about 1820 or so given place to the establishment in the industry of a British style which, nevertheless, from time to time, was influenced by a revival of some almost forgotten alien influence. Thus, at Spodes, more than one Oriental design was applied to stone china which was intended for the homes of the solid and stolid middle class. We have to remember, too, that technical difficulties were things of the past, unless a potter had the ideals of a Billingsley; that interest was transferred to decoration from the ware itself, which was no longer something strange and exotic; and that decorators were trained not only in the factories but in well-established schools of art and design. Everyone was catered for. The wealthy still acclaimed the splendid porcelains of Worcester and Derby, Spodes, Davenports, Mintons and countless others, the middle class were satisfied by fine stone chinas and by Wedgwoods fine earthenwares, and for poor people there was much fine earthenware, a great deal of it well printed in blue and in colours.

In addition to these porcelain-making factories whose later wares have already been considered, we ought first to underline the amazing nineteenth-century versatility of the Spode concern. Every style and every kind of ware was produced, and Spode painting, above all, applied to good shapes, is out-standingly good even when it often had to be larger than life – sometimes over-pretentious – to please the *nouveau riche*.

At Rockingham, near Swinton, a well-established earthenware factory made a fine bone-ash porcelain between 1820 and 1840, under the patronage of Earl Fitzwilliam. Lovely tea-services were made, decorated with good ground colours of green, buff and grey, with gilding, in conjunction with careful flowers and landscapes. Unfortunately, and possibly as the result of the patron's insistence, a series of large vases most elaborately and expensively modelled and decorated, and the making of enormous services culminating in one for William IV which is said to have cost £5,000, proved to be ventures so extravagant that the factory was closed down. Of the less ambitious wares the collector may choose between simple porcelain figures characterised by the prolific use of a particularly dark – mazarine blue, pastille-burners and cottages decorated with carefully applied flowers and moss (including the prized ones made in a lavender paste), and a series of charming little dogs and sheep.

The name of Minton will always be held in high regard if only because of the much prized *pâte-sur-pâte* wares, introduced into the factory by M. L. Solon of Paris, in which many successive layers of white slip upon a blue or sage-green ground were used to give an effect like that of a Limoges enamel.

We may admire too the perfected Minton turquoise, used effectively in conjunction with white *Parian* and fine gold, particularly upon dessert services with elaborate cupid-mounted comports. The Parian body was similar to that invented by Spodes in 1846, in an attempt to rival the lovelier Derby biscuit, and it was used to make a considerable number of figures and busts.

Among the many fine bone-ash porcelains of the nineteenth century that made by Davenports of Longport holds a high place, though in the absence of marks it is difficult to identify. Some exceedingly fine dessert services were made, upon which we find coloured grounds of Reckitt's Blue, celadon green and *Rose Pompadour*, with landscape and flower painting.

We have already mentioned the Martin brothers, whose stoneware broke new ground, and who have been acclaimed as the first of the studio potters. So far as porcelain is concerned, Bernard Moore successfully experimented with flambé glazes of the Chinese kind, and with lustres and other original glaze effects. The later company of Moore Bros. made a very distinctive white porcelain decorated in gold with applied lotus flowers and leaves, hops, and other flowers. Colours were also used for applied blackberries and other fruits, and a fine turquoise ground-colour is often seen. Moore's white porcelain is mostly decorative, comprising comports, vases, bowls, menu-holders, candlesticks, clocks, and so on. Glaze effects were the preoccupation also of the Smethwick (Birmingham) *Ruskin Pottery*, owned by the brothers Edward Richard and Howson Taylor. No two pieces are alike, and the ware is of fine quality. Admittedly, the products of both Bernard Moore and the Ruskin Pottery are very late, and were made well into the present century, but like so many other wares of comparable date, they are good enough to be the antiques of the future.

There is no space here to list the many other potters and potteries, working from about 1880 onwards, who were inspired not only by old styles but by the teaching of such men as William Morris, who was the arch-apostle of good design and restraint in decoration of all kinds. More and more interest is indeed being taken in their wares, which are being steadily collected, and which are beginning to command high prices accordingly.

PLATE 167   Spode Jardinière. A
late piece, of the Copeland era,
made about 1879, richly gilded.
It was painted by the master of
all Spode artists, C. F. Hürten.

PLATE 168   Set of Spode Vases.
Under Josiah Spode the Second,
who died in 1827, many splendid
patterns, such as this which was
numbered (and marked) *2575*,
were introduced. The ground is
gros-bleu, allied to fine mercury
gilding, and effective use was made
of 'pearled' borders in white in the
Sèvres style.

PLATE 169 Spode Tray. The painter of this dish, the design of which is a throw-back to the years when the exotic bird was so popular, is unknown, but he worked at the end of the nineteenth century. The panel is set in turquoise enamel, bearing flowers and leaves in raised, tooled gold; the scrolls upon the 'frame' are similarly treated.

PLATE 170 Rockingham Pot-Pourri Vase. The illustration cannot shew the lovely yellow-green ground colour, but the romantic style of landscape-painting, with a castle framed by trees, is a feature of Rockingham vases. The gilding on this specimen is particularly fine.

PLATE 171 Rockingham Vase. At the time when this vase was made, about 1830, the same technique of applied-flower decoration was used at Coalport, and it is often difficult to distinguish between the wares of the two factories. However, apart from certain differences in the forms and colours of the flowers used, a reliable pointer is often the presence of the raised yellow and gilded scrollwork that may be seen here above the base and around the cover.

PLATE 173   Martin Ware Vase.   A salt-glazed stoneware base in the more restrained Martin Ware style, decorated with an incised pattern of fish and sea plants on a fawn ground. It was designed and made by the Martin brothers at their Southall workshop, and is marked *8-87*.

PLATE 172   Pair of Minton Vases.   These vases were made in 1871, and were decorated by Marc Louis Solon, a Sèvres artist, who introduced at Minton's the *pâte-sur-pâte* technique. In this technique translucent, white or tinted, porcelain slip was painted and modelled on a stained Parian body, in this case on dark-blue panels, on a green ground. He worked very much in the manner and style of T. J. Bott of Worcester, and was probably inspired by the beauty of Limoges enamels.

PLATE 175 Worcester Tazza. The later Worcester paste has a beauty which needs little adornment. This tazza, of the Kerr and Binns period, bearing the shield mark for 1859, was painted by J. Rushton and gilded by S. Ranford. Rushton was one of the factory artists singled out to make copies of fine paintings provided by the management.

PLATE 174 Worcester Vase. Wares in the Persian style quickly followed those in the 'Japanesque' taste, and many were pierced in a manner which was developed to a very high standard at Worcester. This vase is double-walled, and made in the famous 'ivory' body. The modelling was by . Hadley (who left to found his own small factory in the city), and the decoration of the small panels, in gold, was done by S. Ranford.

PLATE 176 Rockingham Basket. Dating
to about 1830–40 this basket is typical of the
lovely specimens made at Rockingham,
Worcester, Coalport and Longport
(Davenport factory).

PLATE 177 Spode Figure. One of
the few figures made by Spodes; it dates
to about 1800, and is marked *SPODE* in red.
The piece is six inches in height, and is
remarkable for its modern style, vigorously
yet economically modelled, and effectively
decorated with conventional flowers. This
kind of figure shews a marked departure
from the copies of continental models
which were produced by the early factories.

PLATE 178 De Morgan Tile. A typical example of William de Morgan's work in his 'Persian' colours. This fine flowing design of a lion rampant was carried out at his Fulham Sands End Pottery, *circa* 1888–98. The tile is marked with a Tudor rose and *William de Morgan & Co. Sands End Pottery, Fulham,* and is three feet six inches by two feet eight and a half inches.

INDEX

Plate numbers are shown in bold face type

255